Peacekeeper's Guide to Firearm Fundamentals

Master the Basic Firearm Fundamentals 2nd Edition

Nicholas Cooley, Ph.D.

Peacekeeper's Guide to Firearm Fundamentals
Master the Basic Firearm Fundamentals

Nicholas Cooley, Ph.D.

All rights reserved. No portion of this book may be reproduced, photocopied, stored, or transmitted in any form except by prior approval of the author or the publisher, except as permitted by U.S. copyright law.

Published by "Dr. Nicholas Cooley, PhD."

Printed in the United States of America

U.S. Copyright © 2026 CI-38755975321

ISBN: 978-1-7366069-0-2

DISCLAIMER

The information in the book is sound advice based on years of experience in firearm training. The author is certified by dozens of organizations. The book's information does not represent any organization that the author is a member or certified by. The author recommends that each person seek formal professional training by a Certified Firearm Instructor.

DEDICATION

This book is dedicated to all responsible firearm owners who understand that ownership is not merely a right, but a profound responsibility. It is for those who value safety above all else, who commit to continuous learning, and who recognize the importance of ethical conduct. My sincere gratitude extends to the countless individuals, from seasoned professionals to new enthusiasts, who have shared their experiences, insights, and dedication to the principles of safe and effective firearm use. Your commitment to excellence and your unwavering adherence to safety are the true inspiration behind this work. May this guide serve as a valuable resource in your pursuit of knowledge and mastery, fostering a community of informed, capable, and exceptionally responsible firearm stewards. This dedication also extends to the educators and mentors who have shaped my understanding and practice, passing down wisdom and experience that forms the bedrock of effective instruction. Their influence is woven into every page, aiming to equip you with the knowledge and mindset to be a true 'peacekeeper' in your own right, upholding the highest standards of safety and proficiency.

PREFACE

In a world where responsible firearm ownership is often met with misunderstanding, this book, "Peacekeeper's Guide to Firearm Fundamentals," aims to cut through the noise with clarity, precision, and an unwavering commitment to safety and proficiency. My journey into the realm of security, emergency services, and firearms instruction has been a long and deeply educational one, spanning decades of hands-on experience and rigorous academic pursuit. It has become abundantly clear that true competency with firearms is not born of mere access, but of dedicated understanding, disciplined practice, and a profound respect for the power and responsibility that accompanies them. This guide is born from that understanding, distilled from countless training sessions, real-world applications, and a deep dive into the behavioral science that underpins human performance under pressure. We will navigate the essential principles of firearm safety, from the cardinal rules to practical application, and explore the fundamentals of marksmanship with a methodical approach, ensuring that each reader, regardless of their current skill level, can build a robust foundation. This is not simply a manual on how to shoot; it is a comprehensive approach to responsible firearm stewardship, encompassing legal considerations, secure storage, and the lifelong commitment required to maintain peak competency. My hope is that this book equips you with the knowledge, confidence, and ethical framework to become a safe, proficient, and conscientious firearm owner.

CONTENTS

Chapter 1 The Foundation of Responsible Firearm Ownership 11
   Understanding Your Why Defining Your Needs 11
   Firearm Selection Matching Tool to Task 19
   The Importance of a Thorough Test Fire 31
   Legal and Ethical Consideration Before Purchase 43
   Building Your Initial Firearm Toolkit 52

Chapter 2: Unwavering Commitment to Firearm Safety 61
   The Cardinal Rules of Firearm Safety 61
   Expanding Safety Practical Checklist for Real World Scenarios 69
   Safe Handling Transferring and Receiving Firearms 80
   Range Etiquette and Procedural Safety 88
   Identifying and Clearing Common Malfunction 97

Chapter 3: Secure Storage and Environmental Protection 109
   The Ethical Imperative of Secure Storage 109
   Choosing the Right Firearm Safe, Size, Security and Access 116
   Leveraging Locking Devices for Everyone Security 124
   Ammunition Storage Safety and Environmental Control 135
   Environmental Considerations for Firearm Preservation 143

Chapter 4: Mastering the Fundamentals of Marksmanship 153
   The Pillars of Accuracy Primary Marksmanship Fundamentals . 153
   Stance The Stable Platform for Precision 162
   Grip Control and Consistency 169
   Trigger Control and the Smooth Break 177

Follow Through Completing the Shot Cycle 186

Chapter 5: Advance Marksmanship and Situational Proficiency 196

Sight Alignment and Sight Picture Achieving Precision Aim 196

Breathing Control for Steady Aim 207

Understanding and Utilizing Eye Dominance 214

Proficiency of One Handed Shooting 226

Introduction to Malfunction Drills and Reloading Techniques ... 234

Chapter 6: The Lifelong Commitment to Firearm Competency 245

Continuous Training the Path to Mastery 245

Legal Preparedness Navigating the Law with Confidence 252

Mental Readiness and Emotional Control 258

Selecting a Qualified Instructor Investing in Your Skill 267

The Responsible Firearm Owners Pledge 275

Appendix 282

Comprehensive Firearm Safety Checklist 282

Acknowledgements 302

Glossary 303

References 304

Author Biography 305

Contact the Author 308

INTRODUCTION

The term "firearm fundamentals" might evoke images of the shooting range, the crisp report of a shot, and the satisfying thud of a bullet hitting its mark. While these are indeed components, the true fundamentals of firearm ownership extend far beyond the physical act of firing. They are rooted in a deep and abiding respect for the tool itself, an unshakeable commitment to safety, and a clear understanding of the responsibilities that accompany the decision to own and operate a firearm. This guide, the "Peacekeeper's Guide to Firearm Fundamentals," is meticulously crafted to provide responsible individuals with the comprehensive knowledge and practical skills necessary for safe and effective firearm handling. My background, blending decades of practical security experience with advanced academic study in fields ranging from behavioral science to business administration, has allowed me to synthesize complex information into accessible, actionable insights. We will delve into the foundational 'why' behind firearm ownership, ensuring your choices are informed and deliberate. We will rigorously examine the non-negotiable principles of firearm safety, integrating them into your daily habits and mindset. Furthermore, we will meticulously break down the core marksmanship skills, emphasizing the subtle yet critical nuances that separate casual proficiency from true mastery. This book is designed for those who seek not just to own a firearm, but to understand it, respect it, and wield it with the utmost competence and ethical consideration. It is a journey toward becoming a true peacekeeper, armed with knowledge and guided by responsibility.

CHAPTER 1

The Foundation of Responsible Firearm Ownership

Understanding Your Why Defining Your Needs

The journey into responsible firearm ownership begins not with the selection of a firearm, but with a deep, introspective examination of purpose. Before a single grip is felt, a single caliber considered, or a single manufacturer researched, lies the fundamental question: why do you desire to own a firearm? This introspective "why" is the bedrock upon which all subsequent decisions will be built. Without a clear understanding of your motivations and intended applications, you risk making choices driven by impulse, peer pressure, or the allure of marketing, leading to a firearm that is ill-suited for your needs, potentially compromising safety and effectiveness. This foundational self-assessment is not a mere formality; it is a critical prerequisite to informed, responsible ownership.

Let's delve into the common motivations that lead individuals to consider firearm ownership. Understanding these will help you identify with one or more and articulate your own specific objectives.

One of the most prevalent reasons is home defense. For many, the presence of a firearm in the home is seen as the ultimate deterrent and a means of protecting oneself and loved ones from potential intruders. When considering home defense, several critical factors come into play. What is the layout of your home? What are the potential points of entry? Do you have children or other vulnerable individuals in the household? The answers to these questions will influence the type of firearm that might be most suitable. For instance, a firearm intended for home defense might prioritize ease of use under stress, reliability, and sufficient stopping power. Accessibility is also a key concern; the firearm must be readily available in a true emergency, yet securely stored to prevent unauthorized access. This necessitates a careful balance between immediate availability and robust safety measures. The tactical considerations of engaging a threat within the confines of a home are vastly different from those in an open field. Understanding distances, potential for collateral damage, and the legal framework surrounding the use of deadly force in self-defense are all integral parts of this "why." This isn't about becoming a vigilante; it's about ensuring you have the means to protect your sanctuary should the worst-case scenario unfold.

Another significant motivation is sport shooting and recreational use. This broad category encompasses a wide range of activities, from casual plinking at an outdoor range to more formal target shooting competitions. For some, the appeal lies in the challenge of precision, the pursuit of accuracy, and the satisfaction of mastering a skill. This might involve disciplines like precision rifle shooting, where extreme accuracy at long distances is paramount, or perhaps action pistol sports, which test speed, accuracy, and tactical movement. The requirements for a firearm used in sport shooting can vary dramatically. A competitive trap shooter will have very different needs than someone who enjoys shooting .22 caliber rifles for fun. Factors such as recoil, ergonomics, ammunition cost, and the specific rules of a particular shooting discipline will heavily influence the choice. If your primary "why" is sport, consider what kind of shooting interests you most. Are you drawn to the discipline of bullseye shooting, the fast-paced nature of practical shooting disciplines, or the quiet focus of long-range marksmanship? Each of these paths will lead you to different types of firearms and accessories. The understanding of these differing needs is vital in guiding your selection toward a tool that will enhance, rather than hinder, your enjoyment and progress in your chosen sport.

Hunting is a traditional and deeply ingrained reason for firearm ownership for many. This practice connects individuals with the outdoors, provides sustenance, and is often a cherished activity passed down through generations. When considering hunting, the choice of firearm and caliber is directly dictated by the game being pursued and the regulations governing hunting in your area. A firearm suitable for hunting small game, like squirrels or rabbits, will be vastly different from one needed for large game such as deer, elk, or bear. Factors like bullet trajectory, energy transfer, ethical harvesting practices, and the firearm's ability to withstand rugged outdoor conditions become paramount. Furthermore, understanding the specific hunting seasons, local wildlife management laws, and the ethical responsibilities associated with taking a life are as critical as understanding the firearm itself. A hunter must be proficient not only with their weapon but also with fieldcraft, tracking, and the proper field dressing of game. The "why" of hunting extends beyond mere marksmanship; it encompasses a respect for nature, a commitment to conservation, and a deep understanding of the ecosystem.

Collecting is another valid reason for firearm ownership, driven by historical interest, aesthetic appreciation, or the pursuit of rare and unique pieces. This motivation often focuses on the craftsmanship, historical significance, or design of firearms. A collector might be interested in antique firearms, military service weapons, or firearms from specific manufacturers or eras. For the collector, the "why" might be less about practical application in a self-defense scenario or a shooting sport and more about preservation, appreciation, and the acquisition of items of value, be it monetary, historical, or personal. While the primary focus here might not be on immediate utility, the principles of safe storage and responsible ownership remain absolutely non-negotiable. A collector must still adhere to all applicable laws, ensure firearms are stored securely, and understand the inherent dangers associated with any firearm, regardless of its intended purpose or value. The passion for collecting can be immense, but it must always be tempered with an unwavering commitment to safety and legality.

Beyond these common motivations, there are other, perhaps less frequent, but equally valid reasons for firearm ownership. This might include professional use, such as for licensed security personnel, law enforcement officers, or those involved in specialized fields where firearms are a required tool of their trade. For these individuals, the "why" is intrinsically linked to their professional responsibilities and often involves rigorous training and adherence to strict protocols. Their needs will be highly specific and dictated by the requirements of their profession.

It's also important to acknowledge that sometimes, the initial "why" might be influenced by external factors. Perhaps a friend is passionate about shooting, or a particular movie portrayed firearms in a heroic light. While these influences are understandable, it's crucial to move beyond them and establish your *own* genuine purpose. Owning a firearm is a significant responsibility, and it should stem from a well-thought-out personal decision, not from conforming to external pressures or romanticized notions.

Once you begin to articulate your "why," you can start to identify the specific characteristics you'll need in a firearm. If your primary concern is home defense, you might be looking for a firearm that is relatively easy to operate under stress, has a manageable recoil, and is reliable. This might lean towards a semi-automatic pistol with a certain capacity, a pump-action shotgun, or a carbine-style rifle. The size and weight might be less of a concern if the firearm is primarily kept in a secure location within the home, but ease of handling and maneuverability in tight spaces could be important.

Conversely, if your "why" is competitive shooting, the specific discipline will dictate your needs. For precision rifle competitions, you'll need a firearm known for exceptional accuracy, potentially with adjustable stock, specialized triggers, and the ability to mount sophisticated optics. For action shooting sports, a reliable semi-automatic pistol with a good trigger and a comfortable grip, perhaps with modifications for speed and handling, might be ideal. Ammunition cost and availability also become significant factors when considering high-volume practice for competitive events.

For hunting, the "why" becomes incredibly specific. For small game, a .22LR rifle or a rimfire pistol offers low recoil and economical ammunition, ideal for practice and smaller targets. For larger game, the caliber must possess sufficient energy to humanely and effectively dispatch the animal at typical hunting distances. This often means venturing into calibers like .308 Winchester, .30-06 Springfield, or even larger magnums for the biggest game. The firearm itself needs to be durable, reliable in various weather conditions, and potentially capable of being carried long distances in the field.

The collector's "why" might lead them to seek out firearms based on rarity, historical significance, or aesthetic appeal. This could involve anything from a vintage Colt Single Action Army revolver to a World War II service rifle, or even a finely engraved sporting shotgun. The primary criteria here are often provenance, condition, and historical context, rather than purely practical performance.

Understanding your "why" is not a one-time exercise. As you gain experience and your interests evolve, your reasons for owning a firearm may shift or expand. The responsible owner is one who regularly re-evaluates their needs and ensures their firearm ownership remains aligned with their current purposes and ethical obligations.

This foundational step of defining your "why" is the most critical part of the entire process. It prevents impulsive purchases, ensures that you acquire a tool that is appropriate for its intended use, and sets the stage for making informed decisions regarding selection, training, and safe storage. By taking the time to honestly assess your motivations, you are laying the groundwork for a safe, responsible, and fulfilling relationship with firearm ownership. This introspective work is an investment in yourself, your safety, and the safety of those around you. It is the responsible starting point for anyone embarking on this path, and it is the commitment that will guide every subsequent decision you make. Without this clear articulation of purpose, you are essentially navigating without a map, susceptible to getting lost in a sea of options and potentially making choices that you will later regret. Embrace this self-discovery; it is the cornerstone of true firearm competency and responsibility.

Firearm Selection Matching Tool to Task

The journey from understanding your "why" to actually holding a firearm in your hands is a critical one, demanding careful consideration of the tool itself and how it aligns with your identified purpose. It's about matching the right instrument to the task at hand, ensuring both effectiveness and safety. This isn't a decision to be made lightly, nor should it be driven by aesthetics or the latest trends. Instead, it's a pragmatic approach to selecting a reliable partner in achieving your goals, whether that's protecting your home, excelling in a sport, ethically harvesting game, or appreciating historical craftsmanship.

When we talk about firearm selection, several fundamental characteristics come into play, each with its own set of implications. The first, and often most debated, is caliber. This refers to the diameter of the bullet, and by extension, the cartridge it is housed in. Caliber directly influences the firearm's power, recoil, and the availability and cost of ammunition. For home defense, calibers like 9mm Luger for pistols or .223 Remington/5.56 NATO for carbines are popular choices. They offer a balance of manageable recoil, sufficient stopping power, and widespread availability of ammunition, which is crucial for both practice and potential real-world scenarios. In contrast, hunting larger game demands more potent calibers. For instance, a deer hunt might necessitate a .308 Winchester or .30-06 Springfield, while hunting larger, more dangerous game like elk or bear might require even more powerful options such as a .300 Winchester Magnum or a .375 H&H Magnum. The selection here is not just about making a larger hole, but about delivering adequate energy transfer to humanely and effectively neutralize the target at hunting distances. For sport shooting, the caliber choice is often dictated by the specific discipline. .22 Long Rifle is a perennial favorite for precision practice, plinking, and certain competitive events due to its low cost, minimal recoil, and inherent accuracy. Larger calibers are used in disciplines requiring more power and range, such as long-range shooting or some pistol competitions. Collectors might be drawn to specific calibers associated with historical firearms, regardless of their modern practical utility.

Equally important is the action type of the firearm. This describes how the firearm loads, fires, and ejects a spent cartridge. The most common types include revolvers, semi-automatic pistols, semi-automatic rifles, pump-action shotguns, and bolt-action rifles. Revolvers, known for their simplicity and reliability, typically hold fewer rounds than semi-automatics but are often considered very robust and less prone to certain types of malfunctions.

Their manual of arms is straightforward, which can be advantageous under stress. Semi-automatic pistols, the most prevalent choice for self-defense and law enforcement, use the energy of the fired cartridge to cycle the action, automatically ejecting the spent casing and loading a new round from a magazine. This allows for a higher rate of fire and greater ammunition capacity than revolvers. Semi-automatic rifles, like the AR-15 platform or AK-47 variants, offer similar advantages in terms of capacity and rate of fire, making them popular for sport shooting and home defense. Pump-action shotguns are a classic choice for home defense and hunting, valued for their reliability and versatility in using various ammunition types (loads). The manual action of pumping the fore-end to cycle the weapon provides a tactile confirmation of operation. Bolt-action rifles are the workhorses of precision shooting and hunting. They require the user to manually operate a bolt to chamber a new round and extract the spent casing. This manual operation, combined with their inherent mechanical simplicity, often contributes to exceptional accuracy and reliability, making them ideal for situations where follow-up shots are deliberate and precise.

The size and weight of a firearm are crucial considerations, particularly when it comes to ergonomics and handling.

For home defense, a firearm that is too large or heavy can be cumbersome, especially for individuals with smaller stature or less upper body strength. A compact pistol or a lighter carbine might be more manageable than a full-sized rifle or a heavy shotgun. Ease of manipulation – racking the slide on a pistol, operating the bolt on a rifle, or manipulating the action on a shotgun – is paramount. If you cannot comfortably and reliably perform these actions under duress, the firearm's effectiveness is severely compromised. For concealed carry, size and weight are even more critical, requiring smaller, lighter firearms that can be discreetly carried. For hunting, the weight of a firearm becomes significant when it needs to be carried for extended periods through varied terrain. A lightweight bolt-action rifle can be a much more practical choice for a backcountry hunt than a heavy sniper rifle. Similarly, in sport shooting, the balance and ergonomics of a firearm can significantly impact shooter comfort and performance over long shooting sessions or during dynamic movements. A well-balanced rifle or pistol can reduce fatigue and improve accuracy.

Beyond these core attributes, reliability is non-negotiable. A firearm, regardless of its caliber or action type, is only useful if it functions consistently when needed. This is where the reputation of the manufacturer and the specific model comes into play. Choosing firearms from established companies with a proven track record of producing reliable products is a wise investment in your safety and your confidence. Researching reviews, consulting with experienced shooters, and understanding the inherent design philosophies of different manufacturers can provide valuable insight. Some firearms are known for their robust simplicity, while others might offer more advanced features but potentially at the cost of complexity. The "best" firearm is one that is both reliable and appropriate for your needs, not necessarily the most feature-rich or expensive.

It is also vital to consider the intended environment where the firearm will be used. A firearm intended for the rugged, wet conditions of a waterfowl hunt will need to be built differently than a firearm destined for a climate-controlled indoor range. Corrosion resistance, material durability, and resistance to environmental factors like dirt and moisture are all important. For home defense, the potential for over-penetration through interior walls is a significant concern. This leads to discussions about ammunition choice, but also about the firearm itself. A handgun firing a lighter, faster projectile might present a different risk profile than a high-powered rifle round. Understanding these nuances is part of responsible ownership.

When it comes to hands-on evaluation, nothing replaces actually handling different firearms. Visiting reputable gun stores is an invaluable step. Don't be intimidated. Engage with the staff, ask questions, and express your intended uses. Many stores will allow you to hold firearms, feel their weight, assess their balance, and check how the controls operate. Pay attention to how the grip fits your hand, whether you can easily reach the trigger and safety mechanisms, and how the firearm points naturally. For many, shooting a firearm is the ultimate test. If possible, visit a local shooting range that offers rentals. This allows you to experience the recoil, the trigger pull, and the overall shooting dynamics of various models before making a purchase. This direct experience can quickly reveal whether a firearm feels "right" in your hands and whether its performance meets your expectations. Some ranges also offer introductory courses or have instructors available who can guide you through trying different types of firearms.

The selection process should also account for your physical capabilities. Can you comfortably manipulate the slide on a semi-automatic pistol? Can you manage the recoil of a particular caliber? Do you have the strength to effectively operate a pump-action shotgun? These are not minor questions; they are fundamental to safe and effective firearm use.

If a firearm is too challenging for you to operate reliably, it is not the right firearm for you, regardless of its other merits. Similarly, consider the maintenance requirements. Some firearms are designed for simpler cleaning and maintenance, while others may require more specialized knowledge or tools. For a new owner, starting with a firearm that is relatively easy to maintain can build confidence and ensure that routine upkeep is performed diligently.

Let's delve deeper into specific firearm types and their common applications.

Pistols:

Revolvers: Often chambered in calibers like .38 Special, .357 Magnum, or .44 Magnum. Their simplicity and reliability make them a favored choice for self-defense and some hunting applications (e.g., .44 Magnum for medium game). They are generally less concealable than semi-automatic pistols due to their cylinder.

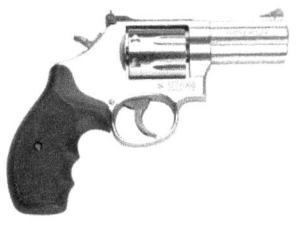

Semi-Automatic Pistols: The most common type, available in a vast array of calibers (9mm, .40 S&W, .45 ACP, etc.) and sizes. Compact and subcompact models are popular for concealed carry, while full-sized models are often preferred for home defense and range shooting due to their greater magazine capacity and often softer recoil. Their modularity allows for customization with accessories like lights and optics.

Rifles:

Bolt-Action Rifles: The standard for precision shooting and hunting. They offer excellent accuracy and reliability. Common calibers range from the small .22LR to powerful magnum cartridges for large game. Their manual operation ensures a controlled cycling of the action, which is ideal for deliberate shots.

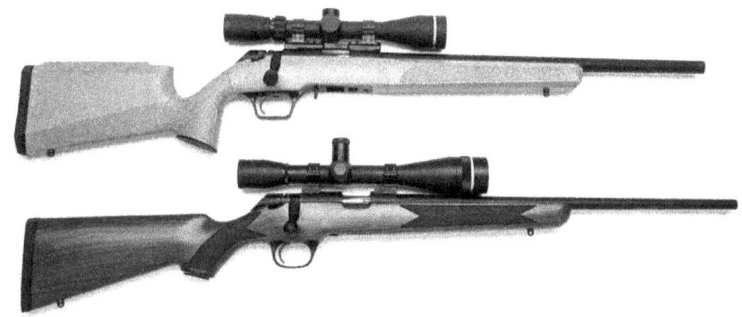

Semi-Automatic Rifles: Platforms like the AR-15 and AK-47 are incredibly popular for sport shooting, home defense, and some hunting. They offer faster follow-up shots and higher capacity magazines.

Caliber choices are extensive, with .223 Remington/5.56 NATO being ubiquitous for AR-15 style rifles, while AK platforms often use 7.62x39mm.

Lever-Action Rifles: A classic American firearm, often

chambered in calibers like .30-30 Winchester or .35 Remington. They are well-suited for hunting in dense woods where shots are typically at moderate ranges and faster follow-up shots might be desired. Their classic aesthetics also appeal to collectors.

Carbines: These are essentially shorter-barreled versions of rifles, designed for greater maneuverability. They are excellent choices for home defense and some types of sport shooting, offering a balance of manageable size and rifle-like performance.

Shotguns:

Pump-Action Shotguns: A versatile and reliable choice for home defense, hunting, and sport shooting (like skeet and trap). They can fire a variety of loads, from birdshot to buckshot to slugs, offering flexibility. Their manual operation is straightforward and dependable.

Semi-Automatic Shotguns: Offer a higher rate of fire and softer recoil than pump-actions, making them popular for sporting clays and waterfowl hunting. They use the energy of the fired shell to cycle the action.

Break-Action Shotguns (Single and Double Barrel): Typically used for hunting and clay sports. Their simplicity and reliability are key features. Double-barreled shotguns offer the ability to load two different types of shells, or to have two shots available before reloading.

When considering **manufacturers**, a few names consistently rise to the top due to their long-standing reputation for quality and reliability. For pistols, brands like Glock, Smith & Wesson, Sig Sauer, and CZ are widely respected. In the rifle market, manufacturers such as Ruger, Savage, Remington, and various

AR-15 producers (e.g., BCM, Daniel Defense, Aero Precision) are well-regarded. For shotguns, companies like Remington, Mossberg, Benelli, and Browning have a strong heritage. However, it's crucial to remember that even the most reputable manufacturers can have individual models or batches that present issues, and conversely, less common manufacturers can produce excellent firearms. This reinforces the importance of researching specific models and reading reviews.

The process of firearm selection is an iterative one. You begin with your "why," which guides you toward certain categories of firearms. Then, you explore the specific characteristics within those categories—caliber, action, size, and weight—considering your physical capabilities and the intended environment. Finally, you engage in hands-on evaluation and research to find a specific model from a reliable manufacturer that best fits your needs. This methodical approach ensures that your firearm is not just a purchase, but a carefully chosen tool, suited for its purpose and wielded with responsibility. It is the practical realization of your foundational understanding of firearm ownership.

The Importance of a Thorough Test Fire

The contemplation of selecting a firearm—whether for home defense, sport, hunting, or collecting—is a significant undertaking. We've discussed caliber, action, ergonomics, and manufacturer reputation.

Yet, even with the most thorough research and diligent handling of a firearm in a retail environment, there remains an element that can only be truly understood through live fire. This is the crucial step of the test fire, a practical evaluation that bridges the gap between theoretical knowledge and visceral experience. It is the moment where the nuances of recoil management, the feel of the trigger under actual firing conditions, and the inherent accuracy of the firearm are brought to life, offering insights that no amount of reading or dry practice can fully replicate. To approach firearm ownership responsibly means committing to this vital evaluative step, ensuring that the tool you choose not only meets your needs on paper but also performs to your satisfaction and comfort when it matters most.

The act of firing a projectile from a firearm is a dynamic event, involving an intricate interplay of forces and sensations. When a cartridge is discharged, it generates a significant amount of energy. This energy propels the bullet down the barrel, but it also results in several other phenomena that directly affect the shooter. Recoil is perhaps the most immediate and noticeable of these. It's the backward and upward momentum of the firearm that results from the forward thrust of the bullet and expanding gases. The perceived recoil is a complex equation, influenced by factors such as the caliber of the ammunition, the weight of the firearm, the design of the muzzle brake or compensator (if present), and the shooter's grip and stance. A firearm that feels manageable and pleasant to shoot in a controlled environment might become a challenging beast to handle when subjected to repeated firing if its recoil is poorly managed or too substantial for the individual. Similarly, a firearm with a relatively light recoil impulse might feel different under the stress of a live-fire scenario than it did during a brief handling session. Experiencing this firsthand allows you to gauge your personal tolerance for recoil and your ability to maintain control of the firearm through multiple shots. This is not merely about comfort; it's fundamentally about control and the ability to accurately deliver subsequent shots if necessary. A shooter who is overwhelmed by recoil is less likely to achieve accurate follow-up shots, which can be critical in defensive situations or competitive shooting.

Beyond recoil, the trigger is the primary interface between the shooter's intent and the firearm's action. While you can practice trigger control through dry firing, the actual sensation of a trigger breaking under the pressure of a live round is a distinct experience. A crisp, clean trigger pull can significantly enhance accuracy, allowing the shooter to maintain their sight picture until the moment of discharge.

Conversely, a gritty, heavy, or mushy trigger can lead to unintentional movement of the firearm as the trigger is pressed, resulting in shots that deviate from the intended point of aim. Some triggers, especially in defensive firearms, are designed with a heavier pull weight for safety reasons. Others, particularly in competition or precision shooting, are designed to be lighter and crisper. Experiencing different trigger types in live fire is essential for understanding which is most conducive to your shooting style and accuracy requirements. You might discover that a particular firearm's trigger, which felt acceptable during a quick press in a store, becomes a significant impediment to accuracy when you have to consciously manage its pull during a string of fire. This is where the "feel" of the firearm truly comes into play, extending beyond its external dimensions and into the mechanics of its operation.

Accuracy, of course, is the ultimate goal of most firearm use. While a firearm might be inherently accurate, its actual precision in the hands of a particular shooter is a combination of the firearm's capabilities and the shooter's ability to exploit them. A test fire allows you to assess how well you can shoot a specific firearm. Are you able to consistently place shots within a desired area? Does the firearm's sight system align well with your vision?

Does the grip facilitate a stable shooting platform for you? These are questions that can only be answered by sending rounds downrange. Many shooting ranges offer rental firearms, providing an excellent opportunity to try out various models and calibers before committing to a purchase. This is an investment in your satisfaction and effectiveness. Trying a 9mm semi-automatic pistol you've been considering is one thing; feeling its balanced weight, the crispness of its trigger, and the way it settles back into your hand after a shot is another entirely. You might find that a particular model, despite its positive reviews, simply doesn't "point" naturally for you, or that its sights are difficult for you to acquire quickly. These are subtle, yet critical, factors that surface only during live fire.

The process of engaging in a test fire requires careful preparation and a commitment to safety. Foremost, always ensure you are at a certified shooting range or a designated safe area where discharging a firearm is permitted and supervised. Never attempt to test fire a firearm in an uncontrolled environment. When you arrive at a range that offers rentals, explain your intended purpose for the firearm to the range officer or instructor. This will help them recommend suitable firearms for you to try. For instance, if you're looking for a home defense handgun, they might suggest a standard-sized 9mm pistol from a reputable manufacturer known for reliability. If you're interested in a hunting rifle, they might offer models in calibers appropriate for the game you intend to pursue.

When you are presented with a firearm for testing, conduct a thorough visual inspection, just as you would with a firearm you were considering purchasing. Ensure it is unloaded, verify the action is clear, and examine it for any obvious signs of damage or wear. Pay attention to the cleanliness and functionality of the moving parts. Before you even begin shooting, familiarize yourself with the basic operation of the firearm: how to load it, how to safely engage and disengage any external safety mechanisms, how to properly grip it, and how to aim. If you are unfamiliar with the firearm's controls, ask the range staff for a demonstration.

The actual shooting process should be approached systematically. Begin with a few shots to acclimate yourself to the firearm and its recoil. Focus on your fundamental shooting principles: stance, grip, sight alignment, sight picture, trigger control, and follow-through. It can be incredibly beneficial to have an experienced instructor present during your test fire. They can observe your shooting technique, identify any issues you might be having with the firearm, and offer constructive feedback. For example, an instructor might notice that you are flinching due to anticipation of recoil, or that your grip is causing the firearm to shift during firing. They can then provide guidance on how to correct these issues, allowing you to get a more accurate assessment of the firearm's potential performance.

What should you be observing and evaluating during a test fire? Make a mental checklist of key aspects:

Recoil Management: How does the firearm feel in your hand as it recoils? Are you able to control the muzzle rise? Can you easily bring the sights back onto the target for a follow-up shot? Does the recoil feel manageable for your physical capabilities, or is it jarring and uncomfortable? Consider the difference between shooting a lightweight .45 ACP pistol and a heavier 9mm. The perceived recoil can be substantially different, and this is a critical factor for sustained shooting or for individuals with less upper body strength.

Trigger Feel and Performance: Is the trigger pull smooth, or does it have a gritty or spongy feel? Is the reset of the trigger discernible, meaning you can feel and hear when it's ready to fire again? Does the trigger contribute to accurate shooting, or does it make it difficult to keep the sights steady? Pay attention to the trigger weight; while you can't change it easily on many firearms, you can learn if a particular weight is suitable for your needs and skill level. For defensive firearms, a slightly heavier trigger pull can be a safety feature.

Ergonomics and Handling: How does the firearm fit your hand? Can you comfortably reach the controls, such as the magazine release and slide stop? Does the firearm point naturally meaning that when you bring it up to eye level, your sights are already aligned with your target? This "pointability" is a subjective but crucial aspect of firearm selection. Some grips might be too large or too small for your hand, affecting your ability to maintain a firm and consistent grip.

Reliability: This is paramount. Did the firearm function flawlessly during your test? Were there any malfunctions, such as failure to feed, failure to eject, or stovepipes? While a short test fire might not reveal all potential reliability issues, it can certainly expose any immediate problems. A firearm that jams during a test fire is a significant red flag. You are looking for smooth, uninterrupted operation.

Accuracy: Are you able to shoot the firearm accurately? This depends on your skill, of course, but also on how well the firearm's sights align with your eye, and how well you can manage its trigger and recoil.

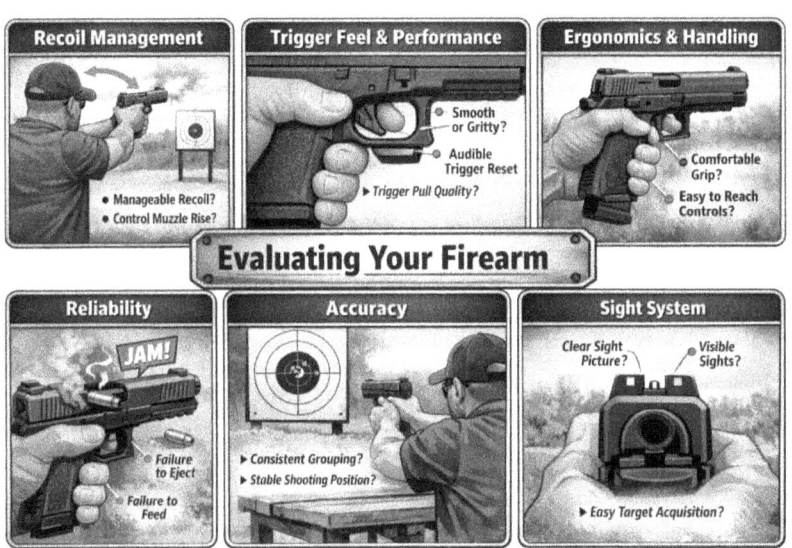

Try to shoot from a stable position, such as a bench rest if available, to eliminate as many variables as possible and get a true sense of the firearm's inherent accuracy. Then, try shooting from a standing position to simulate more practical scenarios.

Sight System: How easy is it for you to acquire the sights and achieve a proper sight picture? Are the sights clear and well-defined? Some firearms come with fixed sights, while others have adjustable sights. Some shooters prefer fiber optic front sights for better visibility in various lighting conditions, while others prefer plain black sights. Your test fire is the ideal time to evaluate the factory sights or to get a feel for what type of aftermarket sights might be beneficial.

When you are assessing a firearm for home defense, the recoil and the ease of control are particularly important. You need a firearm that you can confidently operate under duress. For a first-time owner, a firearm with manageable recoil and straightforward operation is often preferable, even if it means a slight compromise in rate of fire or magazine capacity compared to a more advanced model. The ability to shoot accurately and reliably is far more important than having the highest capacity magazine if you cannot control the firearm.

For sport shooting, the focus might shift slightly. Accuracy and trigger feel become even more critical. If you're participating in precision shooting disciplines, you'll want a firearm that allows for consistent and tight shot groups. For dynamic shooting sports, a firearm that is fast to shoot, easy to transition between targets, and has a quick reset trigger might be more advantageous.

For hunting, reliability in various weather conditions, accuracy at range, and manageable weight for carry become paramount.

A test fire can help you understand how the rifle handles off hand, how it feels when shouldered repeatedly, and how its recoil affects your ability to make precise shots.

It's important to acknowledge that a brief test fire at a range may not perfectly replicate the high-stress environment of a true self-defense situation. However, it provides an invaluable baseline. It allows you to develop muscle memory, understand the firearm's handling characteristics, and build confidence in your ability to operate it safely and effectively. This confidence is a critical component of responsible firearm ownership. A firearm that feels alien or intimidating in your hands, even after practice, is less likely to be used effectively, and may even introduce an element of fear or hesitation that is counterproductive.

When renting firearms for testing, it's wise to try a variety of models that fit your intended purpose. If you are considering a particular semi-automatic pistol, try a few different brands and sizes. If you are looking at a bolt-action rifle, try different stocks and barrel lengths. Even within the same caliber, firearms can feel and perform quite differently. This comparative experience is invaluable. Don't be afraid to ask the range staff for their opinions or to observe other shooters, provided it's done safely and without disruption.

The cost of ammunition and range time should be factored into your overall firearm acquisition budget. Think of it not as an expense, but as a necessary investment in making the right choice. A few boxes of ammunition and a couple of hours at the range can save you from purchasing a firearm that you ultimately find unsuitable, saving you both money and potential frustration in the long run. It is far more cost-effective to spend a modest amount on testing a few firearms than to purchase one that you later have to sell at a loss or, worse, never become proficient with.

Furthermore, a test fire can help you identify any physical limitations you might have that could affect your firearm choice. Perhaps you find that operating the slide on a particular semi-automatic pistol is too difficult for your hands. This information is crucial and will guide you towards firearms with different operating mechanisms or features, such as ambidextrous controls or slides that are easier to manipulate. Similarly, if you find the recoil of a certain caliber to be excessively punishing, you can then focus on firearms chambered in more manageable calibers that still meet your performance requirements.

Ultimately, the test fire is the practical application of all the research and consideration you've undertaken. It's the moment of truth where theory meets reality.

By engaging in this process thoughtfully and safely, you are not only making a more informed purchasing decision but also demonstrating a commitment to responsible firearm ownership. You are ensuring that the firearm you choose is one that you can handle proficiently, one that inspires confidence, and one that is appropriately suited to your stated purpose. This hands-on evaluation is a cornerstone of selecting a firearm that you can use effectively and safely for years to come.

Legal and Ethical Consideration Before Purchase

The journey toward responsible firearm ownership, as we've established, extends far beyond the mechanical aspects of selecting a particular make and model. While understanding the nuances of caliber, action type, and ergonomics is vital, the foundation of this responsibility is firmly rooted in a comprehensive understanding of the legal and ethical frameworks that govern firearm acquisition and possession. To embark on this path without a clear grasp of these principles is akin to navigating treacherous waters without a compass or chart – a recipe for potential disaster, both for oneself and for society. This subsection is dedicated to illuminating these crucial, non-negotiable aspects, ensuring that your pursuit of firearm ownership is both lawful and ethically sound.

At the federal level, the United States has established a foundational set of laws designed to regulate firearm commerce and possession. The cornerstone of this framework is the Gun Control Act of 1968 (GCA), which significantly expanded federal authority to regulate firearms. Central to the GCA is the requirement for federally licensed firearms dealers (FFLs) to conduct background checks on potential purchasers. This is typically facilitated through the National Instant Criminal Background Check System (NICS), operated by the FBI. When you purchase a firearm from an FFL, your identifying information is submitted to NICS, which checks against databases of individuals legally prohibited from possessing firearms. These prohibitions include convictions for felonies and certain misdemeanor domestic violence offenses, those adjudicated as mental defectives or who have been committed to a mental institution, unlawful users of controlled substances, individuals dishonorably discharged from the armed forces, those who have renounced their U.S. citizenship, and those subject to certain restraining orders. It is your absolute responsibility to ensure you do not fall into any of these prohibited categories. Misrepresenting yourself to an FFL to acquire a firearm is a federal crime with severe penalties, including significant fines and lengthy prison sentences.

Beyond background checks, federal law also mandates waiting periods for firearm purchases in certain states, though these vary considerably. While federal law does not impose a universal waiting period, many states have enacted their own laws requiring a specific duration between the purchase of a firearm and its physical transfer to the buyer. These waiting periods are often intended to provide a "cooling-off" period, allowing individuals who may be experiencing temporary emotional distress or who have impulsively decided to acquire a firearm to reconsider. It is imperative to be aware of the specific waiting period laws in your state, as they can directly impact the timeline of your firearm acquisition.

Furthermore, federal law prohibits certain types of firearms and accessories. For instance, machine guns manufactured after May 19, 1986, are generally illegal for civilian possession, with very limited exceptions for highly regulated and expensive registered pre-1986 machine guns. Similarly, unregistered short-barreled rifles (SBRs) and short-barreled shotguns (SBSs) are also prohibited. The National Firearms Act (NFA) governs these and other regulated items, such as silencers (suppressors) and destructive devices, requiring extensive registration, background checks, and a significant tax stamp for legal acquisition.

Understanding these NFA regulations is crucial if you are considering ownership of any such items, as non-compliance carries severe legal ramifications.

It is critical to understand that federal laws establish a baseline, but state laws can be, and often are, far more restrictive. The Second Amendment to the U.S. Constitution, as interpreted by the Supreme Court, protects an individual's right to keep and bear arms, but this right is not unlimited. States have considerable latitude to enact laws that regulate firearm ownership, possession, and use, provided they do not infringe upon the constitutional right. This means that what is perfectly legal in one state may be entirely prohibited in another. For example, some states have universal background check requirements that extend beyond FFL transactions to private sales, meaning that even if you purchase a firearm from a private individual, you may be required to go through an FFL and a background check. Other states have significantly stricter regulations regarding the types of firearms that can be owned, such as bans on certain semi-automatic rifles often referred to as "assault weapons," or restrictions on the capacity of magazines.

To navigate this complex legal landscape, you must become intimately familiar with the laws of your specific state, and often, your local municipality. Ignorance of the law is never a valid defense. This means actively researching your state's firearm statutes. Many state police websites, Attorney General offices, and reputable Second Amendment advocacy organizations provide summaries of state firearm laws. However, for definitive clarity, consulting with a legal professional specializing in firearm law in your jurisdiction is highly recommended, particularly if you have any questions or concerns about your eligibility or the legality of a specific firearm or accessory.

Beyond state and federal statutes, local ordinances can also impose further restrictions. Some cities or counties may have regulations concerning firearm storage, where firearms can be carried (even if open or concealed carry is permitted statewide), or even outright bans on firearms in certain public places. It is your duty to ensure compliance with all applicable federal, state, and local laws. Failure to do so can result in anything from fines and confiscation of firearms to significant jail time and a permanent criminal record, which would then render you a prohibited person under federal law.

The concept of "prohibited persons" is central to firearm law. As mentioned, these are individuals legally barred from owning or possessing firearms due to various factors, including criminal history, mental health adjudications, or specific domestic violence findings. It is not enough to simply not have a felony conviction; you must actively ensure you do not fall into any of the federally or state-defined prohibited categories. If there is any doubt about your eligibility, it is far wiser to seek legal counsel or to refrain from acquiring a firearm than to risk legal repercussions.

Firearm registration is another area where laws vary dramatically. Some states require certain types of firearms, or all firearms, to be registered with the state. Other states explicitly prohibit the registration of firearms by state or local law enforcement agencies. Understanding whether your state requires registration is crucial, as failure to comply with registration laws can have serious consequences.

Ethical considerations are the moral compass that guides responsible firearm ownership, complementing the legal framework. Owning a firearm is not merely a right; it is a profound responsibility. The ethical dimension compels us to consider the potential consequences of our actions and to act in a manner that prioritizes safety, minimizes risk, and upholds the sanctity of human life. Legally owning a firearm does not grant a license to misuse it, to brandish it carelessly, or to resort to its use at the slightest provocation.

The ethical owner understands that a firearm is a tool of last resort, intended for legitimate self-defense and the protection of oneself and innocent others when all other options have been exhausted and there is an immediate, unavoidable threat of serious bodily harm or death.

The principle of self-defense, while legally recognized, also carries a significant ethical weight. The decision to use lethal force, even in self-defense, must be grounded in necessity. This means that you must have reasonably believed that deadly force was necessary to prevent imminent death or great bodily harm to yourself or another innocent person. It implies a duty to retreat if safely possible, though this duty varies significantly by state (e.g., "Stand Your Ground" laws). Ethically, one must always consider if de-escalation, escape, or the intervention of law enforcement were viable alternatives before resorting to the use of a firearm. The ethical owner is trained to assess situations, to avoid unnecessary confrontations, and to prioritize non-violent resolutions whenever feasible.

Furthermore, ethical firearm ownership demands a commitment to the safe storage of firearms. This is not just a legal requirement in many jurisdictions, but an ethical imperative. Firearms must be stored in a manner that prevents unauthorized access, particularly by children, individuals who are legally prohibited from possessing firearms, or those who may be experiencing a crisis. This typically involves using secure safes, locked cabinets, trigger locks, and storing ammunition separately from the firearm. The negligent storage of a firearm that subsequently leads to injury or death of another person, especially a child, is a profound ethical failure with devastating consequences. A responsible owner takes every reasonable precaution to ensure their firearms cannot be accessed by those who should not have them.

The ethical owner also understands that firearm proficiency is a continuous process. It is not enough to simply acquire a firearm; one must dedicate themselves to regular training and practice. This training should cover not only marksmanship but also safe handling, legal aspects of self-defense, and scenario-based training that helps the owner develop sound decision-making skills under pressure. An ethically responsible firearm owner invests time and resources into becoming proficient, ensuring they can operate their firearm safely and effectively if the need ever arises, and crucially, that they can do so without posing an undue risk to themselves or others.

The decision to carry a firearm in public, whether openly or concealed, brings with it an even greater ethical burden.

It means that one is prepared to use lethal force at any moment, and therefore, must exercise extreme caution and judgment in all public interactions. The ethical carrier is constantly aware of their surroundings, prioritizes de-escalation, and understands the severe legal and moral ramifications of any firearm discharge. They are acutely aware that the presence of a firearm on their person introduces a level of potential lethality into any situation, and this awareness must inform every aspect of their public conduct.

In conclusion, before you even consider the physical act of purchasing a firearm, a deep and thorough dive into the legal and ethical considerations is not just advisable, it is absolutely essential. This involves understanding the complex web of federal, state, and local laws governing firearm ownership, including background checks, waiting periods, prohibited persons, and registration requirements. Equally important is embracing the profound ethical responsibilities that accompany the right to bear arms. This includes a commitment to self-defense as a last resort, the imperative of safe storage, the ongoing pursuit of training and proficiency, and a constant awareness of the gravity of carrying a lethal tool. By fully engaging with these legal and ethical principles, you lay the groundwork for responsible firearm ownership, ensuring that your actions are not only lawful but also morally sound, contributing to the safety and security of yourself, your family, and your community. This due diligence is the bedrock upon which all subsequent knowledge and practice in responsible firearm ownership must be built. It is the first, and perhaps most critical, step in a lifelong commitment to firearm safety and stewardship.

Building Your Initial Firearm Toolkit

Before even considering the first live-fire exercise or the formal training course, a responsible firearm owner understands that ownership extends beyond the mere acquisition of the firearm itself. To truly embrace this responsibility, a foundational toolkit of essential accessories and maintenance supplies is an absolute necessity. This isn't about accumulating an arsenal of gadgets; rather, it's about gathering the fundamental items that ensure the safe, effective, and prolonged operational life of your firearm, and critically, your own well-being. Think of it as preparing for a long journey; you wouldn't set off without basic provisions, and the same logic applies to the stewardship of a firearm. This initial toolkit is designed to be practical, affordable, and most importantly, to address immediate needs for maintenance, safety, and effective use.

Foremost among these essential items is a comprehensive cleaning kit. The firearm, regardless of its quality or price point, is a mechanical device that requires regular maintenance to function reliably and safely. Dirt, debris, gunpowder residue, and fouling are inevitable consequences of firing a weapon. If left unattended, these contaminants can lead to malfunctions, reduced accuracy, and in the worst-case scenario, dangerous operational failures. A quality cleaning kit typically includes a few key components. You'll need cleaning rods or cables, which are designed to be passed through the barrel to dislodge fouling. These are often made of steel, brass, or carbon fiber, with carbon fiber and brass being preferred for their reduced risk of scratching the barrel's rifling. Attached to these rods are jags or slotted tips, which hold patches or bore brushes. Bore brushes are typically made of bronze or nylon and are essential for scrubbing out stubborn residue. Cleaning patches, usually made of cotton or a synthetic material, are used with cleaning solvents and lubricants to wipe down surfaces and remove loosened debris. A cleaning solvent is crucial for breaking down gunpowder residue and other fouling. There are various types available, from general-purpose cleaners to specialized ones for copper or lead removal. It's wise to start with a reputable, all-purpose solvent. Finally, a lubricant or gun oil is vital for protecting metal surfaces from rust and corrosion, as well as for ensuring that moving parts function smoothly. A good cleaning kit will also include cleaning cloths or rags for wiping down the exterior of the firearm and potentially some cotton swabs or small brushes for reaching nooks and crannies. When selecting a kit, consider one that is versatile enough to accommodate the types of firearms you anticipate owning, or opt for a universal kit that offers a range of adapters and attachments. Many manufacturers offer well-regarded cleaning kits that provide a good balance of quality and value for the new owner. Don't underestimate the importance of a clean firearm; it's a direct contributor to both safety and reliability.

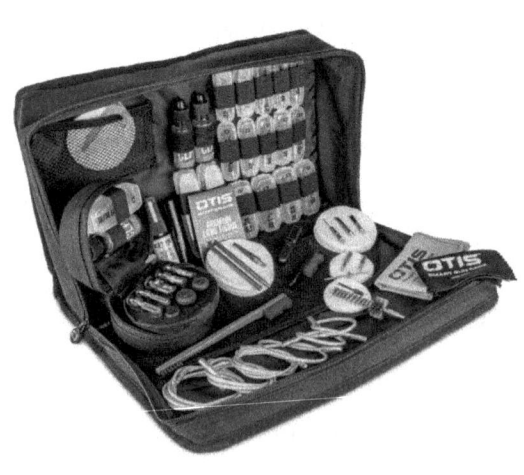

Complementing the cleaning kit are lubricants and gun oils. While many cleaning kits include a basic oil, investing in a high-quality lubricant specifically designed for firearms is a prudent decision. These lubricants are engineered to withstand the extreme temperatures and pressures encountered during firing, providing smooth operation and corrosion protection. There's a spectrum of lubricant types, from traditional gun oils and greases to more modern synthetic formulations. For a new owner, a good quality synthetic gun oil is often an excellent starting point. These oils offer excellent lubrication, resist evaporation, and provide robust corrosion protection across a wide temperature range. Some advanced formulations even contain additives that bond to metal surfaces, providing long-lasting protection and reduced friction. Grease, on the other hand, is a thicker lubricant, often used on high-friction points like slide rails or bolt carrier groups, where it can provide a more durable protective film. For a general-purpose lubricant, however, a good oil will suffice for most needs. Always follow the manufacturer's recommendations for your specific firearm regarding lubrication points and frequency. Over-lubrication can sometimes be as detrimental as under-lubrication, attracting dirt and potentially causing malfunctions, so a light, even application is generally the best approach.

The range is where a firearm truly comes to life, but it's also where safety must be paramount. This brings us to two indispensable items for any firearm owner: protective eyewear and hearing protection. The sound of a gunshot is not merely loud; it is a concussive force that can cause permanent hearing damage with even brief exposure. Repeated exposure, as is common for any shooter, can lead to tinnitus (ringing in the ears) and significant hearing loss over time. Standard earplugs are a minimal start, but dedicated hearing protection is essential. This comes in two primary forms: earplugs and earmuffs. Electronic earmuffs are particularly popular among shooters because they allow you to hear normal conversations and range commands clearly, but instantly suppress dangerously loud noises like gunfire. They are battery-powered and often have adjustable volume controls. Passive earmuffs, while less sophisticated, also offer excellent noise reduction and are a more budget-friendly option. For even greater protection, or when shooting in very loud environments, some individuals opt for custom-molded earplugs, which offer a perfect fit and superior noise attenuation. Regardless of the type chosen, the goal is to reduce the sound pressure level reaching your eardrums to safe levels, typically below 85 decibels (dB).

Equally critical is protective eyewear. Every firearm, even when functioning perfectly, can potentially eject gas, debris, or even small pieces of material. Powder, unburnt propellant, or even a piece of a jacketed bullet can become projectiles. Furthermore, a malfunction can cause parts to break or be ejected. Without adequate eye protection, even a minor incident can result in severe eye injury, potentially leading to blindness. Therefore, wearing protective eyewear every time you handle a firearm, whether at the range, during cleaning, or during any other activity where there's a risk of debris, is non-negotiable. Standard safety glasses with side shields are a minimum requirement. However, dedicated shooting glasses often offer a better, more secure fit and are designed to withstand impacts. Look for glasses that meet the ANSI Z87.1 standard, which signifies they have met rigorous impact resistance requirements. Some shooting glasses also feature interchangeable lenses in various tints, which can improve visibility in different lighting conditions. For instance, amber or orange lenses can enhance contrast, making it easier to see targets against varied backgrounds. Investing in good quality, comfortable eyewear and hearing protection is not an expense; it is an investment in your long-term health and safety.

Finally, the selection of appropriate ammunition is a critical component of the initial toolkit. While it may seem obvious, the importance of using the correct ammunition for your specific firearm cannot be overstated. Firearms are designed to function with specific calibers and types of ammunition. Using the wrong ammunition can lead to catastrophic failures, damage to the firearm, and severe injury to the shooter and bystanders.

First and foremost, you must understand the caliber of your firearm. This information is typically stamped on the barrel or the slide of the gun. For example, if you own a 9mm pistol, you must only use 9mm ammunition. Using ammunition of a different caliber, even if it appears to fit, is extremely dangerous. The internal dimensions of the chamber and barrel are precisely engineered for a specific cartridge. Using an incorrect caliber can result in a failure to fire, a failure to extract, or, in the most dangerous scenarios, a rupture of the chamber or barrel.

Beyond caliber, there are different types of ammunition within a given caliber. For general shooting, practice, and training, full metal jacket (FMJ) ammunition is typically the most common and cost-effective choice. These rounds feature a lead core encased in a copper or copper-alloy jacket. They are designed for reliability and are generally safe for use at most shooting ranges.

For self-defense purposes, Jacketed Hollow Point (JHP) ammunition is often recommended. These rounds have a cavity in the nose designed to expand upon impact, creating a larger wound channel and minimizing the risk of over-penetration, meaning the bullet is less likely to pass through the intended target and pose a risk to bystanders. However, JHP ammunition can be more expensive than FMJ. It's crucial to research and select self-defense ammunition that is specifically recommended for your firearm model, as some firearms can be sensitive to certain types of ammunition, especially JHP.

Ammunition quality also plays a role. While it might be tempting to buy the cheapest ammunition available, especially for practice, extremely low-quality ammunition can lead to inconsistent performance, increased fouling, and a higher risk of malfunctions. Reputable ammunition manufacturers adhere to strict quality control standards. When purchasing ammunition, always check the manufacturer's specifications to ensure it is appropriate for your firearm.

Furthermore, you need to be aware of any ammunition restrictions at the range you plan to frequent. Many indoor ranges prohibit the use of steel-cored or armor-piercing ammunition due to concerns about ricochet and damage to their backstops. Always check the range's rules and regulations before purchasing ammunition for use there.

Finally, ammunition storage is an important consideration. Ammunition should be stored in a cool, dry place, away from heat, direct sunlight, and excessive moisture. It should also be stored securely, out of reach of children and individuals who are legally prohibited from possessing firearms. Many manufacturers sell ammunition in sturdy boxes that are suitable for storage, but for longer-term storage or larger quantities, dedicated ammunition cans are often recommended.

In summary, building your initial firearm toolkit is a foundational step towards responsible ownership. It's about acquiring the essential tools that will enable you to maintain your firearm, protect yourself from harm during its use, and select the appropriate ammunition for safe and effective operation. A quality cleaning kit, reliable lubricants, robust eye and hearing protection, and the correct ammunition are not optional extras; they are fundamental necessities that ensure your journey into firearm ownership begins on a solid footing of safety, reliability, and preparedness. These items represent a modest investment that pays significant dividends in terms of safety, firearm longevity, and your overall confidence and competence as a firearm owner. They are the silent partners that ensure your firearm performs when and how it should, and that you remain safe and sound throughout the process.

Chapter 2:

Unwavering Commitment to Firearm Safety

The Cardinal Rules of Firearm Safety

The journey into responsible firearm ownership, as we've established, begins not with the firearm itself, but with the commitment to safety that underpins its entire existence. We've discussed the essential tools that support this commitment – the cleaning kits, lubricants, protective gear, and the discerning selection of ammunition. Now, we must turn our attention to the most fundamental principles governing the handling of any firearm, principles so critical that they are universally recognized as the cardinal rules of firearm safety. These aren't suggestions; they are non-negotiable tenets that form the bedrock of safe operation, a framework that must be etched into the very consciousness of every individual who interacts with a firearm. They are the guardrails that prevent accidents, the ingrained habits that protect not only the shooter but also everyone in their vicinity.

The first and arguably most crucial of these cardinal rules is: **Treat every firearm as if it were loaded.** This principle is not about assuming a specific firearm *is* loaded; it's about establishing a default mindset that prepares you for any eventuality. Even if you personally unloaded the firearm moments ago, even if you are absolutely certain it is empty, you must maintain this unshakeable discipline. Why? Because mistakes happen. Our minds can wander, memory can fail, and assumptions can be dangerous. A firearm that has been cleared can, through an oversight or a moment of distraction, have a round chamber. By adopting the "treat every firearm as if loaded" mantra, you build in a critical redundancy of safety. This means that before you even touch a firearm, before you examine it, before you move it, your first conscious thought should be about its potential to fire. This mental discipline dictates how you will interact with the weapon. It means you will never point it at anything you are not willing to destroy. It means you will keep your finger off the trigger until your sights are aligned with your intended target and you have made the decision to fire. It means you will be aware of the muzzle's direction at all times. This rule is the foundation upon which all other safety rules are built. It is the unwavering first line of defense against accidental discharge. Think of it as a mental safety switch that is always engaged. Even the most experienced professionals, those who handle firearms daily and have developed a keen sense of their weapons, never deviate from this rule.

It is the ultimate safeguard against complacency, a persistent reminder that a firearm's primary function is to expel a projectile with significant force.

Following directly from the first rule, the second cardinal rule is: **Never allow the muzzle of your firearm to point in a direction that you are not willing to destroy.** This is often referred to as maintaining muzzle discipline. This rule is about understanding and controlling the lethal potential of the firearm. The "direction you are not willing to destroy" encompasses a wide range of possibilities, and its definition must be broad and inclusive. It means never pointing a firearm at another person, even in jest. It means never pointing it at property you value. It means ensuring that even if the firearm were to discharge accidentally, the projectile would strike a safe backstop or a direction where it could cause no harm. This requires constant situational awareness. When you are at a shooting range, the safe direction is typically downrange, towards the designated target. When you are handling a firearm at home, perhaps for cleaning or inspection, the safe direction is paramount. It might mean pointing it towards a solid wall that you know has no one behind it, or towards the floor if that is deemed the safest option in your specific environment, always ensuring your footing and posture do not compromise safety.

This rule demands that you are not only aware of where the muzzle is pointing but also of what lies beyond it. It requires a conscious effort to control the firearm's orientation at all times. Think about the various scenarios: picking up a firearm, setting it down, passing it to another person, drawing it from a holster, or holstering it. Each of these actions requires deliberate attention to muzzle direction. Neglecting this rule can lead to catastrophic consequences. An accidental discharge, even with a seemingly harmless movement, can have devastating results if the muzzle is pointed incorrectly. This is why the combination of the first two rules is so powerful. By treating every firearm as loaded and maintaining strict muzzle discipline, you create a robust safety bubble around the firearm.

The third cardinal rule is perhaps the most critical in preventing accidental firing: **Keep your finger off the trigger and outside the trigger guard until your sights are on the target and you have made the decision to fire.** This rule directly addresses the most common cause of unintentional discharges: premature finger placement on the trigger. The trigger is the mechanism that initiates firing. It requires a deliberate and conscious action. By keeping your finger off the trigger until the exact moment of intended firing, you drastically reduce the possibility of an accidental shot.

This means that as you handle the firearm, as you move with it, as you draw it or present it, your finger should rest alongside the frame, outside the trigger guard. The trigger guard is there to protect the trigger from accidental pressure. Your finger should only enter the trigger guard when you have completed all your preparatory actions, aligned your sights with your intended target, and are mentally committed to firing the shot. This rule is about control and intent. It separates the act of handling a firearm from the act of firing it. It prevents sudden jolts, unexpected movements, or even involuntary muscle spasms from causing the firearm to discharge. Many firearms have triggers that require a specific amount of pressure to activate. However, even light pressure, when applied unexpectedly, can result in a discharge. Some firearms also have very light triggers, which can be desirable for accuracy but can also be more susceptible to accidental activation if this rule is not strictly followed. Think of the process: You acquire the firearm, ensure it is safe and pointed in a safe direction, bring it up to a ready position, acquire your target, align your sights, and *then*, and only then, do you place your finger on the trigger to initiate the firing sequence. This methodical approach, driven by the disciplined adherence to this rule, is paramount.

Finally, the fourth cardinal rule, which underpins the integrity and safe operation of the firearm, is: **Be certain of your target and what is beyond it.** This rule moves beyond the immediate handling of the firearm to encompass the entire context of its use. It is not enough to aim your firearm; you must know precisely what you are aiming at. This requires more than just a visual confirmation. It means understanding the nature of your target and its environment. Are you on a designated shooting range with a secure backstop? Or are you in a situation where the projectile could travel beyond your intended target? This rule is particularly critical in defensive or tactical scenarios, where the target might be moving, obscured, or in close proximity to non-combatants. You must be absolutely certain that the individual or object you are engaging is indeed the threat you perceive it to be, and that beyond that threat, there are no innocent bystanders, pets, or valuable property that could be endangered. This requires keen observation, clear identification, and a comprehensive understanding of your surroundings. In a self-defense situation, for example, a rushed or mistaken identification can have devastating and irreversible consequences. This rule also extends to understanding the projectile's capabilities. Different types of ammunition behave differently upon impact. Full metal jacket rounds can penetrate barriers and continue on their trajectory, while hollow-point rounds are designed to expand and reduce penetration. Understanding these characteristics is part of being certain of what is beyond your target. The goal is to prevent unintended harm. It is about making an informed decision to fire, a decision that is not only justified but also safe in its execution. This involves a constant assessment of the situation, a mental inventory of what lies in the line of fire, and a commitment to only engaging a target when you are absolutely confident in its identification and the safety of the area beyond it.

These four cardinal rules – treating every firearm as if it were loaded, never allowing the muzzle to point in a direction you are not willing to destroy, keeping your finger off the trigger until

ready to fire, and being certain of your target and what lies beyond it – are not abstract concepts.

They are practical, actionable directives that, when internalized and consistently applied, form the unshakeable foundation of firearm safety. They are the rules that separate the responsible firearm owner from the careless one. They are the principles that, through diligent practice and unwavering vigilance, transform from learned behaviors into ingrained habits. At the North Florida Security Academy and through our work at 2A Firearm and Security, LLC, we emphasize that these rules are not merely taught; they are lived. They are reinforced through repetition, scenario-based training, and a culture that prioritizes safety above all else. The goal is to create a mindset where safe handling is automatic, where the mind and body react to any firearm in a way that inherently prevents accidents. This requires a commitment to continuous learning and an understanding that complacency is the enemy of safety. Every time you interact with a firearm, whether it's for training, sport, or for a more serious purpose, these rules must be at the forefront of your consciousness. They are the silent guardians that ensure the tool remains just that – a tool – and never becomes an instrument of unintended tragedy. The conscious practice of these rules, even when handling an unloaded firearm, builds the muscle memory and mental discipline that will serve you when the stakes are highest. It is a commitment to safety that is not just for the range or the training environment, but for every single moment a firearm is present.

Expanding Safety Practical Checklist for Real World Scenarios

The bedrock of firearm safety, as we've deeply explored, is built upon the four cardinal rules. These fundamental tenets are not merely guidelines; they are the non-negotiable principles that every responsible firearm owner must internalize and live by. However, in the complex tapestry of real-world interactions with firearms, abstract rules, while crucial, can sometimes benefit from tangible, actionable frameworks. This is where practical checklists come into play. These structured tools are designed to distill the essence of safe handling into manageable, step-by-step processes, ensuring that critical safety protocols are considered and executed before, during, and after any engagement with a firearm. They serve as a vital reinforcement, especially for those new to firearm ownership who might feel a degree of overwhelm when initially encountering the responsibility. Think of them as a mental safety net, a reminder that ensures no critical step is overlooked, regardless of the situation.

One of the most critical junctures where a checklist can prevent a mishap is before even physically handling a firearm. This "Pre-Handling Checklist" is a mental or even a physically written sequence designed to engage all safety protocols before a firearm is touched. It begins with the absolute foundational step: Confirming the environment is safe for handling. This means ensuring that no unauthorized individuals, particularly children, are present and that the immediate area is free from distractions. Is the firearm in a secure location where it cannot be accidentally accessed? Is there a designated safe direction, and is it maintained even during this pre-handling phase? For instance, if you are about to retrieve a firearm from a safe for cleaning, the checklist would prompt you to first ensure the surrounding area is clear. Then, before touching it, you'd mentally run through the cardinal rules. Is the firearm to be treated as loaded? Absolutely. Is there a safe direction in mind, perhaps pointing it at the floor or a reinforced wall with no one behind it? Yes. Is your finger outside the trigger guard? It must be. This initial mental rigor, reinforced by a checklist, primes the user for safe interaction.

Following the confirmation of a safe environment, the next step in the pre-handling checklist involves the visual and physical inspection of the firearm itself. This is where the "treat every firearm as if it were loaded" rule is put into practice with a methodical approach. The checklist would prompt a thorough examination for any signs of damage or malfunction. Are there any visible cracks in the stock or frame? Is the bore obstructed? Are there any obvious issues with the action? Critically, the checklist must include the step of verifying the firearm is unloaded. This is not a passive assumption but an active, deliberate process. If the firearm is in a case or safe, the checklist dictates that it remains so until you are ready for this verification. When you do begin the verification, the checklist instructs: Keep the muzzle pointed in a safe direction. Keep your finger off the trigger. Cycle the action multiple times, visually and physically inspecting the chamber and magazine well to confirm the absence of ammunition. This isn't just a quick glance; it's a thorough sweep, ensuring that no round is present. For semi-automatic firearms, this involves removing the magazine and locking the slide to the rear, visually inspecting both the chamber and the magazine well. For revolvers, this means opening the cylinder and visually inspecting each chamber. The checklist would emphasize repeating this verification process if the firearm is to be handed to another person or if there's any doubt whatsoever. This active confirmation is the direct application of the first cardinal rule, transforming it into a tangible action.

Once the firearm has been confirmed unloaded and inspected, the pre-handling checklist transitions to the preparation for

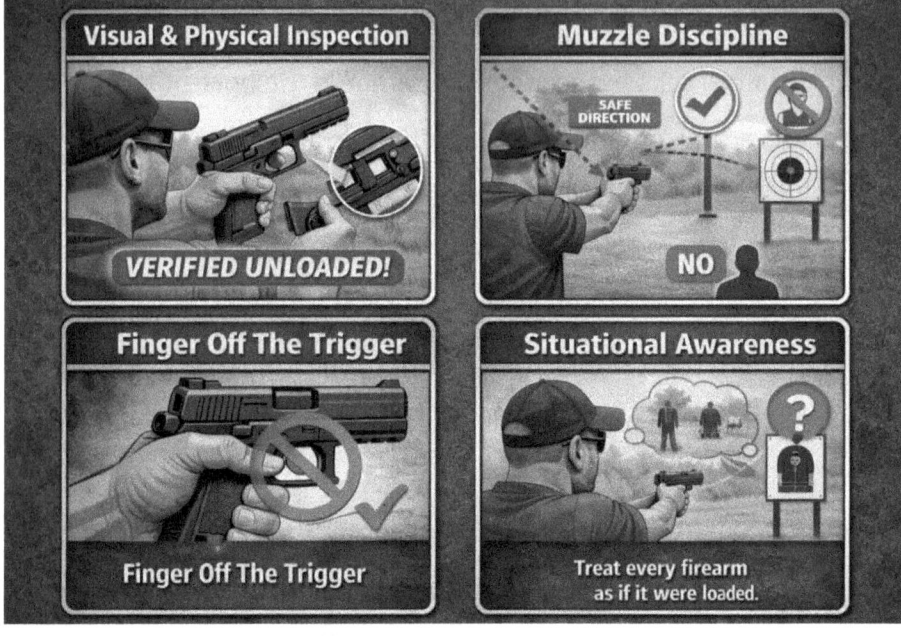

handling. This includes gathering all necessary tools and ensuring they are readily available. If the intention is cleaning, this means having the appropriate cleaning rods, brushes, patches, lubricant, and any specialized tools. If the intention is dry-practice, it means ensuring you have a safe, designated area and potentially snap caps if available. The checklist would prompt: "Are all necessary supplies within easy reach?" "Is the workspace clear of obstructions and designed for safety?" For example, if you're cleaning a handgun at a table, the checklist would ensure there's no clutter that could cause the firearm to be dropped or shifted unexpectedly. It would also reinforce that the firearm, even though confirmed unloaded, should still be kept pointed in a safe direction and your finger should remain off the trigger during this preparation phase. This stage is about setting the stage for a safe and efficient interaction, minimizing the need for unnecessary movement or reaching once the actual handling begins.

Following the pre-handling phase, the next critical set of protocols revolves around the actual manipulation and use of the firearm, encapsulated in a "During-Handling Checklist." This checklist is designed to reinforce the cardinal rules during every movement and decision involving the firearm. The most immediate prompt is the unwavering adherence to maintaining muzzle discipline. As soon as the firearm is picked up, even if confirmed unloaded, the checklist ensures the user is consciously aware of its orientation. Is the muzzle pointed in a safe direction at all times? This is not a static condition; it requires constant vigilance as the user moves. For instance, when moving from a cleaning station to a different part of the room, the checklist prompts a re-assessment of the muzzle's direction. If the firearm is being dry-fired for practice, the checklist emphasizes the importance of a solid backstop, even if no ammunition is present, to ingrain the habit of safe direction.

A significant component of the during-handling checklist is the consistent application of the "finger off the trigger" rule. This is particularly crucial during any movement, transition, or even when pausing during a handling session. The checklist would prompt: "Is your finger indexed along the frame, outside the trigger guard?" This applies whether you are moving the firearm to place it on a cleaning mat, retrieving a tool, or simply repositioning yourself. This habit formation is vital; the goal is to make this the automatic response, so that in a high-stress situation, the finger only enters the trigger guard when the sights are on target and the decision to fire has been made. For example, if during a cleaning session, you need to reach for a different cleaning solution, the checklist would remind you to ensure your finger is off the trigger before reaching, preventing any accidental pressure if your hand jolts or the firearm shifts.

The "During-Handling Checklist" also incorporates situational awareness regarding the target and its surroundings. Even when handling an unloaded firearm for practice or cleaning, maintaining this awareness reinforces a critical mindset. The checklist would ask: "Even in practice, am I aware of what is in the line of fire?" "If this were a live-fire situation, would this be a safe target and backstop?" This mental exercise, even in a controlled environment, helps build the habit of considering the broader context. For instance, if you are dry-firing a rifle in your home, the checklist prompts you to consider the wall behind the target. Is it a load-bearing wall? Are there other rooms on the other side? This reinforces the importance of understanding what lies beyond the immediate action. This extends to knowing the identity of your "target" even in practice scenarios. This might mean practicing identifying threats in a simulated scenario, ensuring that the decision to engage is based on clear identification, a habit that must be cultivated long before it's needed in earnest.

Furthermore, the during-handling checklist addresses the secure and safe manipulation of accessories and ammunition. If a magazine is being inserted or removed, the checklist prompts: "Is the firearm pointed in a safe direction during this action?" "Is my finger off the trigger?" Similarly, if ammunition is present in the vicinity, the checklist emphasizes maintaining separation between the ammunition and the firearm until the deliberate act of loading is intended and performed in a safe environment. For example, when loading a magazine, the checklist would ensure that the firearm itself is secured and not within immediate reach, and that the magazine is being loaded in a controlled manner, again with awareness of the safe direction. This detailed attention to each component and action prevents the common mistakes that can arise from a lack of meticulousness during the handling phase.

Finally, after the direct interaction with the firearm has concluded, a "Post-Handling Checklist" becomes paramount to ensure continued safety and accountability. This checklist focuses on securing the firearm and confirming its unloaded status once more. The first and most crucial step is securing the firearm in its designated safe storage location. This means returning it to a locked safe, a secure cabinet, or another approved method of storage that prevents unauthorized access, especially by children. The checklist would explicitly state: "Is the firearm fully unloaded?" This re-verification is critical. Even if you were meticulous during handling, a final confirmation is the ultimate safeguard. This means repeating the process of visually and physically inspecting the chamber and magazine well. For a handgun, remove the magazine, lock the slide back, and visually inspect the chamber and magazine well. For a revolver, open the cylinder and visually inspect each chamber. This repeated confirmation ensures that the firearm is indeed unloaded before being placed in storage.

The post-handling checklist also includes the crucial step of accountability for ammunition. If any ammunition was handled during the session, the checklist prompts: "Is all ammunition accounted for and secured separately from the firearm?" This means ensuring that loose rounds are collected, magazines are stored appropriately (ideally separately from the firearm, depending on the storage plan), and that no ammunition is left accessible. For instance, if you were loading magazines, the checklist ensures that all loose rounds are collected and returned to their proper storage, and that the loaded magazines are also stored securely. This prevents accidental discoveries by unauthorized individuals later on.

Another vital aspect of the post-handling checklist is cleaning and maintenance verification. If the firearm was handled for cleaning or maintenance, the checklist would prompt: "Is the firearm clean and properly lubricated?" "Are all parts reassembled correctly?" "Is there any remaining cleaning solvent or debris?" This ensures that the firearm is not only safe but also in good working order for its next use. For example, after cleaning a rifle, the checklist would ensure that no patches or cleaning rods are left inside the bore and that the action cycles smoothly.

The post-handling checklist also encompasses personal accountability and debriefing. This involves reflecting on the handling session. Did you follow all safety protocols? Were there any moments of hesitation or uncertainty? Did you encounter any challenges that highlight areas for further training? The checklist might prompt: "Did I maintain focus throughout the entire process?" "Are there any aspects of this session that require additional practice or review?" This self-assessment is crucial for continuous improvement and reinforces the learning process. For instance, if during the handling session, you found yourself rushing a particular step, the post-handling checklist would prompt you to schedule dedicated practice time to master that specific action safely and deliberately.

Finally, the post-handling checklist extends to ensuring the storage area itself remains secure and organized. Is the safe properly locked? Is the key or combination secured? Is the area around the safe clear and unobstructed? This ensures that the overall safety system remains intact. For instance, if the firearm was stored in a case within a larger safe, the checklist would confirm that the case is closed and the safe itself is locked.

These checklists are not intended to be rigid, inflexible dictates but rather adaptable frameworks. The specific items on a checklist can and should be tailored to the type of firearm, the environment, and the specific activity (e.g., home defense, sport shooting, hunting, law enforcement duty). For a firearm intended for home defense, the pre-handling checklist might include a step to "confirm the firearm is loaded (if applicable and safe to do so in the designated area) and in a ready state," whereas for a firearm stored in a safe, the emphasis would be on "confirming unloaded status." The during-handling checklist for a hunter might include "awareness of game animals and non-game animals," while for a competition shooter, it might involve "ensuring compliance with range commands and specific competitive rules."

The key is that these checklists provide a tangible, repeatable process that reinforces safe habits and ensures that critical safety considerations are never overlooked. They serve as a bridge between the understanding of the cardinal rules and their consistent, reliable application in the dynamic and often unpredictable situations that arise in the real world. By integrating these practical checklists into your routine, you are not just learning about firearm safety; you are actively practicing and embedding it into your operational consciousness, creating an unwavering commitment that extends far beyond the moments you are directly interacting with a firearm. They are the practical embodiment of the dedication required for responsible firearm ownership, offering a structured pathway to confidence and security in handling these powerful tools.

Safe Handling Transferring and Receiving Firearms

The secure transfer and reception of firearms represent a critical phase in the lifecycle of firearm interaction, a moment where the responsibility for safety is explicitly handed over and received. This is not a casual exchange, but a deliberate process demanding clear communication, mutual understanding, and rigorous adherence to safety protocols. Whether you are presenting a firearm to an instructor for evaluation, handing it to a certified gunsmith for repair, or receiving one from a peer for inspection, the underlying principles remain constant: safety first, always.

When you are the party initiating the transfer – the one handing over the firearm – the responsibility to ensure it is safe to do so falls squarely upon you. The very first step, before the firearm even leaves your possession, is to confirm it is unloaded. This is not a mere cursory check; it is an absolute, non-negotiable verification. Following the cardinal rules, you must always treat the firearm as if it were loaded until you have personally confirmed otherwise through a deliberate, visual, and physical inspection. This means removing any magazine present, retracting the slide (for semi-automatic pistols and rifles), or opening the cylinder (for revolvers), and visually inspecting the chamber to ensure no round is present. Beyond visual confirmation, a physical check is also paramount. For semi-automatics, cycling the action several times with the slide locked to the rear, while maintaining a safe direction, helps ensure the chamber is clear. For revolvers, opening the cylinder and visually inspecting each chamber, then rotating and repeating, solidifies this verification.

Once you are absolutely certain the firearm is unloaded, the next crucial step is to open the action. For semi-automatic firearms, this typically involves locking the slide to the rear. For revolvers, this means opening the cylinder and ensuring it remains open. This visually communicates the unloaded status of the firearm and provides an immediate, obvious indication that no ammunition can be chambered without deliberate action. This open action is a tangible representation of your commitment to safety and your assurance to the receiving party that the firearm is not loaded. Throughout this entire process, your finger must remain off the trigger and indexed along the frame. The muzzle must, without exception, be pointed in a designated safe direction. This means no sweeping across people, no pointing at the ceiling or floor unless it is the designated safe direction and clear of any potential hazards, and certainly no pointing in a direction where an accidental discharge could cause harm.

When communicating the transfer, clarity and directness are essential. State clearly that you are about to transfer the firearm and that you have confirmed it is unloaded with the action open. For example, you might say, "Instructor, I am now going to hand you this firearm. It is unloaded, and the action is open." This verbal confirmation reinforces the visual cues and ensures there is no ambiguity about the firearm's status. Position the firearm for transfer in a manner that maintains the safe direction. Often, this means presenting it with the muzzle pointed away from both you and the receiving individual, perhaps by holding it by the grip and slide, with the muzzle directed towards a safe area. If you are placing it on a surface for the other person to retrieve, ensure that surface is stable, and the firearm is placed in a way that allows for a safe pick-up.

The responsibility does not end with the transfer; it continues through the moment the other party takes possession. Maintain visual contact with the firearm and the receiving individual until they have a secure grip and have acknowledged its unloaded status. This ensures that no accidental manipulation occurs during the exchange itself. It is a final layer of accountability, ensuring that the safety protocols are maintained through the entire handover.

Conversely, when you are the recipient of a firearm, your role in ensuring safety is equally, if not more, critical. The moment you are about to receive a firearm, you must mentally prepare to assume full responsibility for its safe handling. The person transferring the firearm should have already confirmed it is unloaded with the action open. However, as the receiver, you must never take their word as absolute gospel. Your first action upon taking possession of the firearm, or even as it is being presented to you, is to visually and physically confirm its unloaded status yourself.

Assume the firearm is loaded until you have personally verified it is not. As the firearm is handed to you, ensure that it is presented in a safe direction. If it is not, you have the right, and indeed the obligation, to politely redirect the muzzle to a safe direction before taking possession. Once you have a secure grip, maintain your finger off the trigger and indexed along the frame. Immediately, you must perform your own thorough check. If the action is not open, open it. Remove any magazine that might be present. Visually inspect the chamber and the magazine well for any signs of ammunition. For semi-automatics, cycle the action several times with the slide locked to the rear, visually inspecting the chamber. For revolvers, open the cylinder and inspect each chamber, rotating to ensure all are clear.

This verification process is non-negotiable. It is your ultimate safeguard against a negligent discharge. Even if the person handing you the firearm is a seasoned professional, an oversight can happen. Your diligence protects both yourself and others. Communicate your confirmation to the transferring party. A simple, clear statement like, "Confirmed unloaded, action open," or "I have verified it is unloaded," reinforces the shared understanding of safety.

Beyond the immediate confirmation of an unloaded status, maintaining awareness of the firearm's position and your own actions is crucial. Throughout the reception and initial handling, continue to keep the muzzle pointed in a safe direction. Be aware of your surroundings and any potential hazards. If the firearm is being handed to you for a specific purpose, such as instruction or examination, do not engage in any other activity with it until that purpose is complete and you are ready to re-assess its status for its next phase of handling or storage.

The communication during the transfer and reception of firearms should be a continuous loop. The person handing over the firearm states its status and confirms their actions. The person receiving the firearm acknowledges, verifies, and confirms their own actions. This dialogue leaves no room for assumptions. It is a collaborative effort to ensure that the powerful tool in question is managed with the utmost respect and caution. For instance, imagine a scenario at a firearms training course. The instructor might ask a student to present their firearm for inspection. The student, having been previously instructed, would ensure the firearm is unloaded, the action is open, and then present it to the instructor, stating, "Instructor, this is my firearm. It is unloaded with the action open." The instructor, in turn, would then perform their own verification, perhaps saying, "Thank you. I will now verify the unloaded status," and proceed with their own inspection. This iterative process of confirmation is the hallmark of responsible firearm handling.

Consider the nuances of different types of firearms. Transferring a bolt-action rifle requires ensuring the bolt is open and removed if possible, clearly exposing the chamber. A pump-action shotgun requires the action to be open and the forearm pulled back, and ideally, the magazine tube follower should be visible if it's a removable type, or the action cycled to show it's clear. For all firearms, the principle of visually and physically inspecting the chamber and magazine well remains constant. The "safe direction" might also vary. For a rifle on a shooting bench, the safe direction is typically straight downrange, or if indoors for cleaning, perhaps a solid wall behind the bench. For a handgun during a transfer, it might be a designated safe area on the range, or away from people and towards a safe backstop if the context allows.

The importance of this strict protocol extends to situations involving family members or trusted friends. While a higher degree of trust may exist, the fundamental risks associated with firearms do not diminish. When handing a firearm to a spouse or child (of legal age and appropriate training) for practice, or receiving one from them, the same rigorous steps must be taken. Assumptions about who last handled the firearm or its current state can be dangerous. A simple request to "Please confirm this is unloaded before I take it" or a clear statement of "I am confirming this is unloaded now" reinforces the safety culture. This ensures that the habit of meticulous verification is maintained regardless of the familiarity of the parties involved.

Furthermore, understanding the specific mechanisms of the firearm being transferred is crucial for both parties. The person transferring must know how to safely open the action and confirm it's unloaded on that particular model. The receiver must also be proficient in these actions. If there is any doubt about how to safely clear a specific firearm, it is imperative to seek guidance from a qualified instructor or refer to the manufacturer's manual before attempting to transfer or receive it. Mishandling during this process due to unfamiliarity can lead to serious accidents.

The context of the transfer also dictates certain procedures. For instance, at a controlled shooting range, there will be specific commands and protocols regarding the handling of firearms, including when they can be loaded, unloaded, and transferred. Always adhere strictly to range rules and commands from range officers. They are there to ensure everyone's safety. In a home environment, the protocols might be less formalized but no less critical. If a firearm needs to be handed over for cleaning or maintenance, the same unloaded, action-open, safe-direction rules apply before it is passed to another individual, even if that individual is a family member.

The act of receiving a firearm also requires awareness of what is being done with it subsequently. If you are receiving a firearm to inspect it, you are now responsible for its safe handling during that inspection. If you are receiving it to load it, you must ensure you are in a safe location and following all procedures for loading. This responsibility continues until the firearm is safely stored or actively engaged in its intended purpose under strict safety controls.

In summary, the transfer and reception of firearms are not mere transitions of possession; they are opportunities to reinforce the highest standards of firearm safety. This involves meticulous verification of the unloaded status, clearly communicating the firearm's condition, maintaining a safe direction at all times, and ensuring that both the giver and the receiver actively participate in the safety process. By approaching every firearm transfer with this level of discipline and awareness, you contribute to a culture of safety that minimizes risk and fosters confidence in the responsible ownership and handling of firearms. It is through these deliberate, repeatable actions that the foundation of unwavering commitment to firearm safety is continuously strengthened.

Range Etiquette and Procedural Safety

The shooting range, whether an indoor facility with controlled lighting and ventilation or an expansive outdoor expanse, is a microcosm of responsible firearm handling. It is a shared environment where individuals engage in an activity that, by its very nature, demands precision, focus, and an unwavering adherence to safety. To navigate this environment successfully and to ensure the safety of oneself and every other person present, a deep understanding and consistent practice of range etiquette and procedural safety are paramount. These are not mere suggestions; they are the fundamental pillars upon which a secure and productive shooting experience is built. Ignoring them is not only a disservice to the sport but a direct invitation to disaster.

At the very core of range operations lies the absolute imperative of muzzle discipline. This principle is so foundational that it bears constant repetition and reinforcement. The muzzle of a firearm, under all circumstances, must be pointed in a designated safe direction. What constitutes a "safe direction" can vary depending on the range environment. In an indoor range, it is almost invariably straight downrange, towards the approved backstop. In an outdoor range, it generally means downrange, away from any occupied areas, vehicles, or infrastructure, and never towards the sky, the ground, or any other individual. This rule is inviolable. Even when a firearm is unloaded, and you believe you have taken all necessary precautions, the muzzle's direction must be managed as if a live round were chambered. This means that when moving with a firearm, or when handing it to another individual, or when taking possession of it, the muzzle must remain controlled. Never sweep the muzzle across people, even if you are certain the firearm is unloaded. The habit of maintaining muzzle discipline, even when it seems unnecessary, is the ultimate safeguard against accidental discharges. It becomes an ingrained reflex that can prevent tragedy when the stakes are highest.

Closely linked to muzzle discipline is the equally critical rule regarding the trigger finger. Your finger should only approach the trigger when you are in a safe firing position, aiming at a target, and have made the conscious decision to fire. During all other times – when moving, when loading or unloading, when conversing with others, or when receiving or handing over a firearm – the finger must remain outside the trigger guard, indexed along the frame of the firearm. This simple yet profound rule prevents countless negligent discharges that occur when a finger inadvertently finds its way to the trigger during a moment of distraction, a stumble, or an unexpected movement. Developing the habit of keeping your finger off the trigger, consistently and without exception, is a fundamental step in building a safety-conscious mindset. Think of it as an extension of the firearm's safety mechanism; your disciplined finger is another crucial layer of security.

The flow of activity on a shooting range is often dictated by commands from range officers or safety officers. These commands are not suggestions; they are critical instructions that ensure synchronized and safe operations.

Commands such as "Cease Fire!" or "Stop Shooting!" are unambiguous calls for immediate cessation of all firing. Upon hearing such a command, every shooter must instantly stop shooting, place their firearm on the bench or in a safe position, remove their finger from the trigger, and await further instructions. Similarly, commands related to loading, unloading, or bringing firearms to a ready position are designed to prevent conflicts and manage the flow of the range. Understanding these commands and responding promptly and correctly is not just about following rules; it's about contributing to the collective safety of the entire range. When a "Cease Fire!" is called, assume the worst and react accordingly – stop, clear, and wait.

Shooting bays, whether individual stalls or designated areas, are personal zones of responsibility. While you are on the range, your primary focus should be within your designated area. This means being aware of your immediate surroundings and ensuring that your actions do not impact the safety of adjacent shooters. Never extend your firearm or any part of your body beyond the confines of your shooting bay in a manner that could create a hazard. This includes ensuring that your muzzle is always directed downrange and within the bounds of your designated firing line.

Respecting the boundaries of your shooting bay also extends to managing your equipment and ammunition. Keep your shooting area organized to prevent trips or spills.

The procedural safety of loading and unloading firearms is a cornerstone of range operation. These actions are typically restricted to designated "loading/unloading stations" or to your specific shooting bench, but never in hallways, restrooms, or other common areas. When you are at a loading station or your bench, and you intend to load your firearm, you must first ensure that your finger is off the trigger and that the muzzle is pointed in a safe direction. Open the action of the firearm, insert the magazine or cylinder, and then, and only then, close the action. This sequence ensures that if an accidental trigger pull occurs during the loading process, the firearm is either unloaded or pointed in a safe direction. Conversely, when you are finished shooting or are instructed to unload, always keep the firearm pointed in a safe direction, remove your finger from the trigger, open the action, and visually and physically inspect the chamber and magazine well to confirm it is unloaded. This visual confirmation is critical; never assume.

Ammunition management is another vital aspect of range safety. Ranges often have specific rules about the types of ammunition allowed, and it is essential to be aware of these.

Beyond that, responsible ammunition management means handling it with care and respect. Avoid dropping rounds or magazines, as this can damage them and potentially lead to malfunctions. Always keep ammunition in its designated containers until you are ready to load your firearm. Never handle live ammunition in areas where other shooters are not actively engaged in live fire. This includes not carrying live rounds in your pockets while walking around the range unless you are actively moving to or from a shooting station with the intent to load. When a range officer announces the end of a shooting session, or if you are finished shooting, you should immediately unload your firearm and, if required by range rules, show that it is unloaded by keeping the action open.

The concept of the "safe direction of fire" is the guiding principle for all actions involving a firearm on the range. It dictates where the muzzle must always point. This is not just about preventing harm to people but also about protecting the range infrastructure itself. Firing into the ceiling, the floor (unless specifically designed for that purpose and under controlled conditions), or towards the front of a shooting stall can cause ricochets, damage equipment, and create significant hazards. Understanding the specific design and backstop capabilities of the range you are using is crucial.

Always ensure your firearm is pointed towards the approved target and backstop. If you are unsure about what constitutes a safe direction in a particular scenario, do not hesitate to ask a range officer. It is far better to ask a question than to make a mistake.

Beyond these core principles, there are several layers of etiquette that contribute to a harmonious and safe shooting environment. One such aspect is respecting other shooters' space and concentration. While conversation is often a part of the shooting experience, it should be conducted in a manner that does not distract those who are actively engaged in shooting. Avoid unnecessary noise, sudden movements, or commentary that could disrupt a shooter's focus. When approaching someone who is shooting, do so with caution and wait for a natural break in their activity before engaging them.

Similarly, the proper storage and handling of firearms when not in use are crucial. When you are not actively shooting, your firearm should be unloaded, with the action open, and placed securely in a case or on the bench in a manner that prevents accidental movement. Never leave a loaded firearm unattended on a shooting bench. If you need to step away from your station, even briefly, ensure your firearm is rendered safe and secured. This includes removing magazines and opening the action.

The use of eye and ear protection is not optional; it is mandatory. Firearms produce significant noise levels that can cause permanent hearing damage, and flying debris or ejected casings can cause eye injuries. Always wear appropriate, certified safety glasses and hearing protection (earplugs or earmuffs) while on the firing line or in any area where firearms are being discharged. Ensure your protection fits properly and is worn consistently. Encourage others to do the same.

When you are moving between the parking lot and the range, or moving between different areas of the range, your firearm should always be in a closed, unloaded case. The firearm should only be removed from its case when you are at a designated loading area or your shooting station. This practice prevents any ambiguity about whether a firearm is in use or being transported. It is a clear signal to everyone that the firearm is not being handled or displayed in a public or potentially hazardous manner.

Managing ammunition, particularly during a ceasefire or when leaving the range, requires diligence. Once shooting has ceased, you must unload your firearm and verify it is empty. Any ammunition that has been removed from magazines or boxes should be collected and stored safely. If you are leaving the range, ensure all ammunition is securely stored in a separate container or compartment from your firearm. Never leave loose ammunition lying around, either at your shooting station or in common areas.

The responsibility for safety extends to how you handle your firearm in relation to others. Always be aware of where other shooters are located. If you are moving down the firing line, ensure you do not point your firearm in their direction, even if it is unloaded. When handing a firearm to another person, such as an instructor or range safety officer, follow the established protocols for safe transfer, ensuring the firearm is unloaded and the action is open. Similarly, when receiving a firearm, you have the responsibility to immediately confirm its unloaded status.

Understanding the specific protocols of the range you are visiting is also important. Different ranges may have slightly different rules regarding magazine capacity, types of targets allowed, or specific procedures for ceasefires. Before you begin shooting, take the time to read any posted rules or listen to the range safety briefing. If you are unsure about any rule or procedure, ask a range officer for clarification. It is better to be overcautious and informed than to be unaware and risk an accident.

The mindset of continuous vigilance is key. Shooting is an activity that demands concentration. Treat every firearm as if it were loaded, keep your finger off the trigger until ready to fire, and always point your muzzle in a safe direction. These are not just rules; they are mental disciplines that, when practiced consistently, become second nature. This ingrained safety culture is what allows for a positive and productive experience for everyone on the range. It's about respecting the tool, respecting the environment, and most importantly, respecting the lives of those around you. By embracing these principles of range etiquette and procedural safety, you not only protect yourself but contribute to a culture of responsibility that benefits the entire shooting community. This commitment to unyielding safety standards is the bedrock upon which all proficiency and enjoyment in firearms handling are built.

Identifying and Clearing Common Malfunction

Firearms, like any mechanical device, are susceptible to malfunctions. Despite rigorous quality control and careful maintenance, the complex interplay of components under extreme pressure and heat can, on occasion, lead to an interruption in the firing sequence. Recognizing that such issues can and *do* occur is the first step in addressing them effectively.

It is not a sign of a faulty firearm, nor necessarily a reflection of the shooter's skill, but rather an inherent possibility in a dynamic system. The critical element here is not the occurrence of a malfunction, but the shooter's preparedness and ability to diagnose and resolve it quickly and safely. The principles of firearm safety, particularly muzzle discipline and trigger finger control, become even more paramount during these critical moments. The goal is always to return the firearm to a functional state as rapidly as possible while maintaining a safe direction of the muzzle and keeping the finger off the trigger until the malfunction is cleared and the shooter is ready to re-engage a target.

One of the most frequently encountered malfunctions is the "stovepipe," also known as a failure to eject. This occurs when a spent cartridge case fails to be fully extracted and ejected from the firearm's action. Instead, it becomes lodged at an angle in the ejection port, protruding from the side of the slide or receiver, resembling a stovepipe. The action typically cannot cycle fully, preventing a new round from being chambered and thus rendering the firearm inoperable. When a stovepipe occurs, the immediate instinct might be to repeatedly cycle the action, which can sometimes worsen the problem or even damage the firearm.

The correct procedure, often summarized by the acronym "tap, rack, bang," is designed to address this issue systematically and safely.

The "tap" in this sequence refers to applying firm pressure, or tapping, to the bottom of the magazine. This ensures that the magazine is fully seated, preventing any possibility that a loose magazine is contributing to the problem or might dislodge during the clearing process. While less common for a stovepipe than other malfunctions, it's a good general practice to ensure foundational elements are secure. The more critical action is the "rack." With the muzzle still pointed in a safe direction and your finger off the trigger, firmly pull the slide or charging handle all the way to the rear. This action extracts the stovepiped casing and, upon release, allows the slide to move forward, stripping a new round from the magazine and chambering it. The key here is to perform the "rack" with a decisive and full motion. A limp-wristed or incomplete rack may fail to clear the obstruction. Once the slide has slammed forward, chambering a new round, the firearm is now ready for the "bang." This involves bringing the firearm back on target and, with a controlled press of the trigger, resuming your intended firing sequence.

The entire "tap, rack, bang" maneuver should be executed smoothly and without hesitation, maintaining situational awareness and the core tenets of firearm safety throughout.

Another common and potentially more problematic malfunction is a "failure to feed" or a "double feed." This occurs when a new cartridge fails to be properly chambered in the barrel. In some instances, the firearm's action may attempt to push a new round into the chamber while a previous round (either a live round or a spent casing) is still lodged there. This can result in two rounds attempting to occupy the same space in the chamber, creating a jam. This is often more complex to clear than a stovepipe because the obstruction is internal to the action and may require more than a simple rack.

To address a double feed, the first and most crucial step is to maintain control of the firearm and its muzzle direction. Do not rack the slide. Attempting to rack the slide in a double feed situation can often wedge the rounds more firmly into the action, making them harder to remove. Instead, the firearm needs to be manipulated to remove the jammed cartridges. The exact procedure can vary slightly depending on the firearm platform (pistol vs. rifle), but the general principle involves tilting the firearm to allow gravity to assist in dislodging the rounds.

For many semi-automatic pistols experiencing a double feed, the recommended procedure involves tilting the firearm at approximately a 45-degree angle, muzzle still pointed safely downrange. Then, firmly cycle the slide to the rear multiple times. The tilt, combined with repeated cycling of the slide, helps to dislodge the improperly chambered rounds. You may need to perform this cycling motion several times, potentially tilting the firearm in different directions, until the obstruction is cleared and the slide can move freely forward. Once the slide closes freely, it typically means the jammed rounds have been expelled, and a new round has been successfully chambered. At this point, the firearm can be brought back on target, and the trigger pressed for the "bang." It is essential to visually confirm that the chamber is clear after such a malfunction, if your firearm allows for safe and immediate confirmation without compromising safety.

For semi-automatic rifles, a double feed may present similar, with two rounds trying to enter the chamber. Clearing this often involves rocking the bolt or charging handle back and forth, sometimes in conjunction with tilting the rifle. In some cases, it may be necessary to drop the magazine to help relieve pressure and allow the jammed rounds to be extracted.

Once the rounds are cleared, the magazine is reinserted, the action is cycled to chamber a fresh round, and then the firearm is ready to resume firing. Again, the emphasis must be on maintaining muzzle discipline and keeping the trigger finger off the trigger throughout the entire clearing process. These malfunctions can be stressful, and the tendency to rush or become flustered is natural. However, disciplined, deliberate action is paramount to resolving them safely and efficiently.

Another type of malfunction, less common but significant, is a "failure to extract." This occurs when the firearm cycles (fires and attempts to eject the spent casing), but the extractor fails to grip the rim of the spent casing, or the casing is stuck in the chamber due to excessive pressure or a damaged casing. The result is that the spent casing remains in the chamber or breech, preventing a new round from being chambered. This is often more difficult to clear than a stovepipe because the spent casing is firmly lodged.

To clear a failure to extract, the firearm must be manipulated to physically remove the stuck casing. The first step, as always, is to ensure the muzzle is pointed in a safe direction and the trigger finger is off the trigger. If possible, and depending on the firearm, tilting the firearm slightly can sometimes help to dislodge the casing.

Then, the action (slide or bolt) needs to be cycled to the rear with significant force. The goal is to use the momentum of the action's travel to pull the stuck casing out of the chamber. If a single cycle doesn't work, repeating this forceful cycle may be necessary. Some firearms have specific tools or procedures for clearing difficult extractions, and it's beneficial to be familiar with your specific firearm's capabilities.

In situations where the spent casing is severely stuck, it might even require the use of a cleaning rod or a similar tool to push the casing out from the muzzle end,

after ensuring the firearm is unloaded and the action is open. This is a more involved clearing process and often requires deliberate, firm manipulation. The key is to remain calm, maintain safety protocols, and systematically attempt to clear the obstruction. After the obstruction is cleared and the firearm is confirmed to be ready to chamber a new round, proceed with cycling the action to chamber a fresh cartridge and resume firing.

"Failure to fire" is another potential malfunction, though it is often more accurately described as a failure of ignition. This can happen for several reasons, including a faulty primer in the cartridge, insufficient force from the firing pin, or a mechanical issue with the firearm's ignition system. When you pull the trigger and nothing happens – no bang – the first thing to do is not to immediately assume the firearm is broken. The most critical step here is to adhere to the "wait" principle. Resist the urge to immediately cycle the action or try to fire again.

Instead, keep the firearm pointed in a safe direction, maintain finger off the trigger, and wait for a count of at least 10-20 seconds. This is a safety precaution in case the primer was just slow to ignite, or if a delayed ignition occurs. After this waiting period, if there is still no ignition, you can then proceed to clear the malfunction. The procedure is similar to clearing a failure to extract, as the faulty cartridge is still in the chamber. Cycle the action firmly to the rear to extract and eject the dud round. Once ejected, visually inspect the chamber to ensure it is clear and then chamber a fresh round. The process of bringing the firearm back on target and engaging the trigger for the "bang" then follows.

It is also important to understand that sometimes a malfunction might be caused by a faulty magazine. A damaged magazine, a weak spring, or debris within the magazine can all lead to feeding issues. If you suspect a magazine issue, carefully remove the magazine, inspect it for any visible damage or obstructions, and if possible, try a different, known-good magazine.

If the malfunction ceases with a different magazine, then the original magazine was likely the culprit. Always ensure your magazines are clean and well-maintained.

The techniques described, such as "tap, rack, bang," are fundamental for semi-automatic firearms and are often taught as a baseline for addressing common malfunctions. However, it is crucial to understand the specific operating mechanism of your firearm. Bolt-action rifles, lever-action rifles, and revolvers have different clearing procedures. For instance, in a revolver, a failure to fire might simply mean pulling the trigger again to rotate the cylinder to the next chamber. If multiple chambers fail to fire, then the cylinder needs to be opened, the problematic rounds removed, and the cylinder re-rotated.

Regardless of the specific malfunction or firearm type, several overarching principles should guide your actions:

1. **Maintain Muzzle Discipline:** At all times, the firearm's muzzle must be pointed in a designated safe direction. This is non-negotiable, even during the stress of clearing a malfunction.

2. **Keep Your Finger Off the Trigger:** Your trigger finger should only be on the trigger when you are ready to fire *after* the malfunction has been cleared and the firearm is aimed at a target.

3. **Control the Firearm:** Maintain a firm grip on your firearm throughout the clearing process. This allows for controlled manipulation and prevents accidental movements.

4. **Be Deliberate and Smooth:** While speed is often a desirable outcome, it should not come at the expense of accuracy in your clearing steps. Execute each action with purpose and control.

5. **Know Your Firearm:** Familiarize yourself with the common malfunctions specific to your firearm model and understand the recommended clearing procedures. This knowledge is best acquired through dedicated training and practice.

6. **Practice Malfunction Drills:** Regularly practicing malfunction clearing drills (often called "failure to function" drills) under safe, supervised conditions is essential. This helps to build muscle memory and confidence, enabling you to react effectively and instinctively when a real-world malfunction occurs. These drills should be conducted with an unloaded firearm and dummy ammunition initially, progressing to live fire under instructor supervision.

7. **Visual Confirmation:** Whenever safe to do so, visually inspect the chamber and magazine well to confirm that obstructions have been cleared.

Understanding these common malfunctions and practicing their resolution can transform a potentially dangerous or mission-ending event into a minor, manageable interruption. It is this proactive preparedness, coupled with an unwavering commitment to safety principles, that truly defines a proficient and responsible firearm handler. The ability to diagnose and clear a malfunction under pressure is a testament to training, discipline, and a deep respect for the capabilities and potential complexities of the firearm itself. It underscores the fact that proficiency is not just about accurate shooting, but also about robust and safe firearm management in all circumstances.

Chapter 3:

Secure Storage and Environmental Protection

The Ethical Imperative of Secure Storage

The privilege of firearm ownership in this nation is inextricably bound to a profound ethical and legal responsibility: the secure storage of those firearms. This is not a matter of personal preference or a mere suggestion for the conscientious owner; it is a fundamental duty, a moral imperative that extends far beyond the individual. It is a commitment to the safety and well-being of oneself, one's family, and indeed, the broader community and society at large. The very act of possessing a firearm, a tool designed with destructive capability, places upon the owner an obligation to ensure that this capability is never inadvertently or intentionally unleashed upon those who are not the intended targets, or worse, upon oneself.

When we speak of secure storage, we are talking about erecting a formidable barrier between a firearm and unauthorized access. This barrier is not just physical; it is also a manifestation of a deeply ingrained ethical framework that prioritizes human life and safety above all else. The consequences of failing to uphold this responsibility are stark, tragic, and often irreversible.

The stories that fill the news cycles, the hushed conversations in support groups, and the somber reports from law enforcement agencies all bear witness to the devastating toll that unsecured firearms can exact. Accidental shootings, often involving children who discover a weapon left within reach, shatter families and leave indelible scars. The insidious rise of firearm suicide, where an accessible weapon offers a tragic and impulsive solution to despair, claims far too many lives that might otherwise have been saved with just a few moments of delay, a few more obstacles between the individual and the means to end their life. Furthermore, firearms stolen from unsecured homes or vehicles too frequently find their way into the hands of criminals, becoming instruments of violence in robberies, assaults, and homicides, directly contributing to the cycle of crime and fear that plagues our communities.

To truly grasp the ethical imperative of secure storage, one must internalize the potential ripple effects of negligence. It is not simply about preventing a single incident; it is about mitigating a vast spectrum of risks. Consider the child, driven by innocent curiosity, who stumbles upon a handgun left on a nightstand or a rifle carelessly stored in a closet. Their lack of understanding of the danger, combined with the immediate accessibility of the weapon, creates a scenario rife with peril.

The ensuing accident, though perhaps unintentional, carries the full weight of tragic consequence, a consequence that could have been entirely avoided with responsible storage.

Then there is the individual wrestling with severe mental distress. In moments of acute crisis, the presence of an easily accessible firearm can transform fleeting suicidal ideation into a finalized act. The ethical dimension here is profound: by providing a clear and present means to self-harm, the unsecured firearm becomes an active participant in the tragedy. Secure storage, by introducing even a minimal delay, a moment of deliberation, can provide the crucial window for intervention, for help to arrive, or for the intense emotional storm to pass. It is an act of profound ethical responsibility to create these small, yet vital, pauses that can save a life.

Theft is another critical facet of this ethical discussion. Firearms that are not securely stored are prime targets for burglary. Once stolen, these weapons become potent tools in the hands of individuals who have no regard for the law or human life. The firearm that was legally owned, intended for sport, self-defense, or collection, can be repurposed into an instrument of terror, impacting innocent lives far removed from the original owner. The ethical burden then extends to every crime committed with that stolen weapon.

The owner, through their failure to secure it, bears a moral, and sometimes legal, responsibility for the ensuing violence. This is not about assigning blame for the actions of others, but about acknowledging the direct link between an owner's negligence and the broader societal harm that results.

This understanding of the ethical underpinnings is not intended to instill fear, but to foster a deep sense of purpose and commitment. It elevates the act of secure storage from a mere chore to a vital component of responsible citizenship. When firearms are stored securely, we are actively contributing to a safer environment for our families and our communities. We are demonstrating respect for the power we wield and the responsibility that accompanies it. This ethical foundation is the bedrock upon which all practical firearm storage solutions are built. Without this moral clarity, the most sophisticated safe or lock can be rendered insufficient, as the underlying motivation for their use is absent. It is this ethical imperative that transforms the "how" of secure storage into a truly meaningful endeavor, ensuring that firearms remain tools of responsible use, rather than instruments of unintended tragedy or criminal intent.

The concept of ethical responsibility in firearm ownership is rooted in the fundamental principle of minimizing harm.

Firearms, by their very nature, possess the potential for causing significant injury or death. This potential, while sometimes necessary for legitimate purposes such as self-defense, sport, or law enforcement, also demands an equally significant commitment to preventing their misuse. The ethical owner recognizes this dual nature and acts proactively to mitigate the inherent risks. Secure storage is the primary and most effective method of mitigating these risks when the firearm is not in immediate use. It is a tangible expression of the owner's commitment to protecting others from the potential dangers associated with their property.

Consider the legal frameworks that exist surrounding firearm storage. Many jurisdictions have implemented laws mandating secure storage, particularly when minors have access to the home. These laws, while legal requirements, are also a reflection of a societal understanding of the ethical dangers posed by unsecured firearms. They underscore the collective recognition that preventing accidental shootings and suicides, especially among vulnerable populations, is a shared responsibility. An ethically minded firearm owner will not view these laws as an imposition, but as a validation of their own moral compass, a reinforcement of the principles they already hold dear.

They will strive not just to meet the minimum legal standard, but to exceed it, employing the highest level of security available to them.

The "why" behind secure storage is also deeply intertwined with the concept of trust. When a firearm owner takes diligent steps to secure their weapons, they are, in essence, assuring their community that they are a trustworthy custodian of a potentially dangerous item. This trust is crucial for the continued acceptance and practice of responsible firearm ownership. Conversely, a failure to secure firearms erodes this trust, contributing to negative perceptions and potentially fueling calls for more restrictive measures that may impact responsible owners. The ethical owner understands that their actions have a broader impact on the perception and acceptance of firearms ownership within society.

Furthermore, the ethical imperative extends to considering the mental and emotional state of individuals who may be in close proximity to firearms. A firearm owner has a moral obligation to assess the risk that any individual in their household or with access to their home might pose, either to themselves or to others, if they were to gain access to a firearm. This includes individuals struggling with depression, substance abuse, anger management issues, or any other condition that might impair judgment or increase impulsivity. Secure storage is a proactive measure that creates a necessary buffer, preventing impulsive acts and providing a critical opportunity for intervention.

The act of securing a firearm is, in many ways, an act of preemptive compassion. It acknowledges that life is unpredictable, that emotional states can shift rapidly, and that accidents can happen even to the most careful individuals. By making it difficult for a firearm to be accessed inappropriately, the owner is extending a measure of protection not only to others but also to themselves, safeguarding them from the devastating guilt and consequences that can arise from an avoidable tragedy.

In conclusion, the ethical responsibility for secure firearm storage is multifaceted and profound. It encompasses a commitment to preventing accidental shootings, suicides, and theft. It involves respecting the law, fostering trust within the community, and acting with a proactive and compassionate awareness of the potential risks. By embracing secure storage not as a burden but as a moral obligation, firearm owners fulfill a critical duty, contributing to a safer society and upholding the integrity of responsible firearm ownership. This ethical framework serves as the essential precursor to understanding and implementing the practical measures of secure storage that will be discussed in subsequent sections. It is the driving force that makes these practical measures not just recommended, but absolutely essential for any responsible firearm owner.

Choosing the Right Firearm Safe, Size, Security and Access

The decision to acquire a firearm safe is a pivotal step in responsible firearm ownership, moving beyond the ethical imperatives discussed previously into the practical realm of implementation. This is not a one-size-fits-all endeavor; rather, it demands careful consideration of individual needs, existing collections, and the specific security challenges one aims to address. The market offers a diverse array of secure storage solutions, each with its own strengths and weaknesses, designed to cater to a spectrum of requirements, from the casual owner of a single handgun to the serious collector with an extensive array of firearms. Understanding the nuances of these options is crucial to making an informed choice that provides both robust protection and practical accessibility.

At the most basic level of secure storage, one encounters the **lockbox**. These are typically compact, relatively lightweight containers designed primarily to prevent unauthorized access by children or opportunistic individuals. They are often constructed from steel, though the gauge and quality can vary significantly.

Locking mechanisms on lockboxes are generally simpler, often employing key locks or basic combination dials. While a lockbox can be effective in keeping a firearm out of the hands of the untrained or impulsive, it is generally not considered a high-security solution for protecting against determined theft or environmental hazards like fire. Many lockboxes are designed for portability, making them suitable for securing a handgun within a vehicle or a temporary location, but their limited size and construction may not accommodate larger firearms or offer substantial resistance to sophisticated burglary tools. It is imperative to recognize that a lockbox serves a specific purpose – primarily preventing casual access – and should not be mistaken for a substitute for more substantial security measures when those are warranted.

Moving up in the hierarchy of security and capacity, we find **gun cabinets**. These are typically larger than lockboxes and are designed to store multiple long guns, often with shelving for handguns and ammunition. Gun cabinets are generally constructed from steel, but the gauge and welding techniques can vary considerably. Many lower-end gun cabinets may have thinner steel walls and simpler locking mechanisms, making them more susceptible to being pried open or forced. Higher-quality gun cabinets will feature thicker steel, reinforced doors, and more robust locking systems, offering a significant step up in security from a basic lockbox. However, even a well-built gun cabinet might not offer substantial fire protection unless specifically rated for it. The primary advantage of a gun cabinet over a lockbox lies in its capacity and its ability to keep firearms organized and out of sight, fulfilling a key aspect of secure storage by preventing casual discovery.

The pinnacle of firearm security is the **gun safe**. These are robust, heavy-duty enclosures designed to provide a high level of protection against both theft and environmental damage, most notably fire. Gun safes are constructed from thick steel, often featuring reinforced doors, multi-point locking bolts, and sophisticated locking mechanisms. The quality of construction varies significantly between manufacturers and models, with higher-end safes offering superior resistance to drilling, prying, and cutting attacks. A critical feature of many gun safes is their **fire rating**. This rating, typically expressed in hours (e.g., 30 minutes, 60 minutes, 120 minutes) at a specific temperature (e.g., 1200°F or 1400°F), indicates how long the interior of the safe will remain below a critical temperature that could damage firearms or ammunition. This protection is achieved through the use of specialized insulation materials within the safe's walls and door.

When considering a gun safe, several key construction features demand attention. The **gauge of the steel** used in the construction is a primary indicator of its resistance to forced entry. Thicker steel (lower gauge number) provides greater protection. For instance, 12-gauge steel is significantly more robust than 16-gauge steel. The **door construction** is equally important. A solid steel door with multiple locking bolts extending into the frame on all sides offers far greater resistance to prying than a door with fewer bolts or a simpler hinge system.

Some safes also incorporate **hardened steel plates** or **composite materials** in critical areas, such as around the locking mechanism, to further deter drilling or cutting attacks. The **weight** of a safe can also be an indicator of its security; heavier safes are generally more difficult to move and remove by thieves. However, it's important to note that weight alone is not a definitive measure of security.

The **locking mechanism** is another crucial element in choosing a safe. The most common types include:

Key Locks: These are straightforward and reliable, but they can be susceptible to picking by skilled individuals, and the keys can be lost or duplicated. The quality of the key lock itself varies greatly, with higher-security locks offering better resistance to manipulation.

Combination Locks: These can be either mechanical (dial) or electronic (keypad). Mechanical combination locks are generally considered very reliable and resistant to EMP (electromagnetic pulse) attacks, but they can be slower to open. Electronic locks offer quicker access and the convenience of easy code changes, but they rely on batteries and can be vulnerable to electronic manipulation or failure if not of high quality. Modern electronic locks often feature multiple user codes and audit trails.

Biometric Locks: These utilize fingerprint or other biometric data for access. They offer the fastest access time and eliminate the need to remember codes or keys. However, their reliability can be affected by factors such as dirt or moisture on the scanner, and their long-term durability and security against sophisticated bypass methods are still subjects of ongoing development and debate. It is essential to choose a biometric lock from a reputable manufacturer that has undergone rigorous testing.

When selecting a safe, the **fire rating** should be a paramount consideration, especially if the environment presents a significant fire risk or if the firearms within are of substantial value. It's not enough for the safe to *resist* fire; it must also maintain an internal temperature below the autoignition point of paper and the degradation point of firearm components. Look for safes with U.L. (Underwriters Laboratories) ratings, which are a widely recognized standard for fire endurance. A 60-minute rating at 1400°F is a common benchmark, but longer durations and higher temperature ratings offer superior protection.

Be aware that fire-resistant safes achieve this through insulation, which adds bulk and weight, and can sometimes compromise internal storage capacity.

Beyond construction and locking mechanisms, the **size and internal configuration** of the safe are critical to its practicality and effectiveness. The safe must be large enough to accommodate all current firearms, with room for future acquisitions. Overcrowding a safe not only makes it difficult to access individual firearms but can also lead to damage as weapons shift and bang against each other. Consider the types of firearms you own. Long guns, especially those with optics, require significant vertical space. Handguns can be stored in dedicated racks or drawers. Ammunition, cleaning supplies, and other valuables should also be factored into the storage equation. Many safes offer customizable interiors with adjustable shelves and racks, allowing you to tailor the space to your specific needs.

The concept of **accessibility** is a delicate balance with security. A safe that is so difficult to open that it discourages its use defeats a primary purpose of secure storage, especially in a self-defense scenario. Conversely, a safe that is too easily accessible negates its security function. Therefore, it's important to choose a locking mechanism and a safe design that allows for prompt access when needed, while still presenting a formidable barrier to unauthorized users. For defensive firearms, quick-access features, such as biometric locks or quick-release electronic locks, might be prioritized, but this must be weighed against the overall security profile of the safe and the specific risks present in the household.

The **environment** where the safe will be located also plays a role. If the safe is to be placed in a damp basement or garage, choosing a model with enhanced corrosion resistance or considering a dehumidifier to maintain a dry interior is advisable. Humidity can lead to rust and damage firearms over time. Similarly, if the safe will be in a location prone to extreme temperature fluctuations, this might influence the choice of fire rating and the need for climate control.

The **weight and installation** of a gun safe are also significant considerations. Heavier safes are more resistant to being carried away, but they can also pose challenges for installation, especially on upper floors. Bolting the safe to the floor and/or wall is a critical step in preventing theft. Most quality gun safes come with pre-drilled holes for this purpose, and using lag bolts of appropriate length and strength is essential. Ensure the flooring can adequately support the weight of the safe, especially if it's a large, heavy model.

Finally, the **reputation of the manufacturer** is a crucial factor. Researching brands, reading reviews, and understanding warranty information can provide valuable insights into the reliability and customer support offered. A reputable manufacturer will stand behind their product, offering robust warranties and readily available replacement parts if needed. Investing in a safe from a known and trusted brand is often a wise decision that can pay dividends in long-term security and peace of mind. The initial cost of a quality firearm safe can seem substantial, but when weighed against the potential cost of lost firearms, damage from fire, or the unimaginable tragedy of an accidental shooting or suicide, it represents a prudent and responsible investment in safety and security.

Leveraging Locking Devices for Everyone Security

In the pursuit of comprehensive firearm security, the traditional emphasis often falls upon robust, stationary safes, and for good reason. These formidable enclosures represent the zenith of protection against both theft and environmental threats. However, the practical realities of responsible firearm ownership frequently introduce scenarios where a full-sized, bolted-down safe, while ideal, may not be entirely practical or sufficient on its own. This is where a spectrum of supplementary locking devices comes into play, offering versatile solutions for everyday security needs. These devices, though perhaps less imposing than a vault-like safe, are indispensable tools in preventing unauthorized access, deterring accidental discharges, and ensuring compliance with legal requirements, especially in diverse environments and during transit.

Consider, for instance, the common scenario of a household with children. While a safe is the gold standard for storing firearms when not in active use, the brief period between retrieving a firearm for self-defense and returning it to storage, or the need to temporarily secure a firearm away from immediate reach, presents a critical vulnerability. Similarly, individuals who frequently travel with their firearms, whether for competition, hunting, or professional duties, require locking mechanisms that offer a layer of security during transit and in temporary locations. It is in these interstitial spaces of firearm ownership that smaller, more portable locking devices prove their immense value, acting as vital deterrents and safeguards.

One of the most widely recognized and accessible forms of firearm locking devices is the **trigger lock**. These devices are designed to physically obstruct the firearm's trigger mechanism, thereby preventing the firearm from being discharged. They typically consist of a metal or hardened plastic shackle that encloses the trigger guard and a locking mechanism that engages to prevent the trigger from being pulled. Many trigger locks come with a key, requiring a specific key to disengage and remove the lock. Others utilize a combination mechanism, offering keyless convenience.

The primary advantage of a trigger lock lies in its simplicity and relatively low cost. They are widely available at most sporting goods stores and online retailers, making them an easily obtainable security measure. For many, they represent a minimal barrier that can prevent an impulsive or accidental discharge, particularly by a curious child who might access an unsecured firearm. Their compact size also means they can be easily stored when the firearm is in use.

However, the limitations of trigger locks are significant and should not be overlooked. Firstly, the effectiveness of a trigger lock is entirely dependent on its proper installation. If not fitted snugly around the trigger guard, or if the locking mechanism is not fully engaged, it can be bypassed with relative ease.

More importantly, trigger locks do not prevent the firearm from being handled, pointed, or manipulated. A determined individual, or even a child who is unaware of the firearm's loaded status, could still pick up the weapon, potentially causing distress or injury if the firearm were to be accidentally discharged in a manner unrelated to the trigger itself (though this is extremely rare with modern firearms). Furthermore, the type of trigger lock must be compatible with the specific firearm. Some trigger locks may not fit certain trigger guard shapes or sizes, and in some cases, poorly designed trigger locks can even damage the firearm's finish. It is also crucial to remember that the key for a trigger lock must be kept securely away from the firearm and out of reach of unauthorized individuals, lest the lock itself become a mere inconvenience rather than a security measure.

Another common and often more robust option is the **cable lock**. Similar in concept to a bicycle lock, a cable lock consists of a steel cable, often coated in plastic or rubber to prevent scratching the firearm, which passes through the action of the firearm and is secured by a locking mechanism, typically a key lock or a combination lock. The cable is usually threaded through the ejection port and out the muzzle, or through the magazine well and out the action.

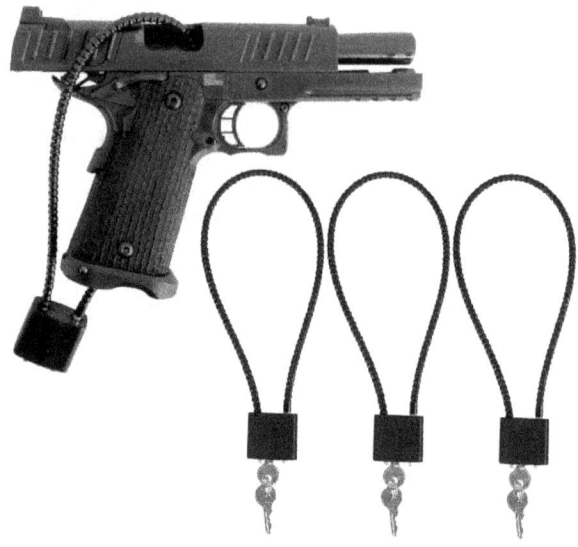

Cable locks offer a more comprehensive level of security than many trigger locks because they physically obstruct the firing mechanism by preventing the action from cycling. This means the firearm cannot be loaded, chambered, or fired while the cable lock is in place. This added layer of prevention makes them a preferred choice for many in situations where the firearm is being stored for extended periods or where there is a greater concern about unauthorized manipulation. Like trigger locks, cable locks are relatively inexpensive and widely available, and their flexibility allows them to be used on a wide variety of firearms, from handguns to long guns.

Yet, cable locks also have their drawbacks. The primary concern is their potential to interfere with proper storage or handling.

If the cable is not fully disengaged and removed before attempting to load or fire the firearm, it can cause damage to the firearm or the lock itself. It is absolutely critical that the user habituates themselves to removing the cable lock as the *very first* step upon picking up a firearm for any purpose, including practice, cleaning, or defense. Misplacing or losing the key to a cable lock can be a significant inconvenience, rendering the firearm temporarily unusable until the lock can be bypassed or removed by a locksmith, which itself can be a costly and time-consuming process. Additionally, while the cable itself is robust, the locking mechanism can vary in quality. Cheaper cable locks may have less secure key mechanisms that are more susceptible to picking or force. The coating on the cable, while protective, can eventually wear down, leading to potential scratches on the firearm's finish if not carefully managed.

A more specialized locking device for handguns is the **pistol grip lock**, sometimes referred to as a grip safety lock or a trigger guard lock. These devices are designed to clamp onto the grip of the handgun and often extend a mechanism that blocks the trigger or the firing pin mechanism. They are typically made of hardened steel and are often more robust than simple trigger locks that attach only to the trigger guard.

The advantage of a pistol grip lock is that it can offer a higher degree of security by engaging more deeply with the firearm's core mechanisms. They are often designed to be difficult to remove without the key and can deter unauthorized handling effectively. Their secure fit around the grip can also make them feel more integrated with the firearm than a simple trigger lock.

However, pistol grip locks, like other devices, have their limitations. Their primary drawback is their limited compatibility. They are designed for specific handgun frame sizes and shapes, and a lock designed for a full-size pistol may not fit a compact or subcompact model, or vice versa. This requires careful selection to ensure a proper fit. Furthermore, while they block the trigger or firing pin, they still do not prevent the firearm from being picked up and manipulated. As with all keyed locks, the security of the pistol grip lock is only as good as the security of its key. If the key is lost or falls into the wrong hands, the security is compromised. Some models can also be cumbersome to attach and detach, which might be a deterrent for those who prioritize rapid access to their firearm for self-defense.

Beyond these common categories, there are other emerging or specialized locking devices. Some firearms come equipped with integrated locking mechanisms, such as a key-operated internal lock that disengages the firing mechanism. These are often built into the firearm's design and can be a secure, albeit limited, option. However, their effectiveness and ease of use can vary greatly by manufacturer. Additionally, some manufacturers offer specialized locks that integrate with the firearm's sights or other components.

It is crucial to understand that these supplementary locking devices are not intended to be a singular solution for all firearm security needs. They are most effective when used in conjunction with other security practices and, ideally, as a secondary layer of security in addition to a properly secured safe. For instance, a handgun stored in a safe might also have a trigger lock or cable lock applied as an extra precaution, especially if there are children in the home or if the safe itself is not designed for rapid access.

The principle of layered security is paramount. Imagine a series of barriers, each designed to thwart unauthorized access or handling. A safe is the primary, most substantial barrier. A trigger lock, cable lock, or pistol grip lock acts as a secondary or tertiary barrier. Even if a thief were to breach the primary barrier (the safe), these secondary locks would still present an obstacle, potentially delaying them long enough to be discovered or to prevent them from immediately using the firearm. In a home environment, the primary goal is to prevent access by unauthorized individuals, especially children. These devices, while not foolproof, add significant friction to a child's ability to access and potentially misuse a firearm.

When choosing and using these devices, several best practices should be adhered to:

1. **Compatibility:** Always ensure the locking device is specifically designed for the firearm you intend to secure. Trying to force an incompatible lock can damage the firearm and compromise security.

2. **Proper Installation:** Read and follow the manufacturer's instructions meticulously. A poorly installed lock is essentially an unlocked firearm. For cable locks, ensure the cable is threaded correctly and that the lock mechanism is fully engaged. For trigger locks, confirm they are securely seated over the trigger guard.

3. **Key Management:** The key to any of these locks must be stored in a location that is secure and inaccessible to unauthorized individuals. This means not in a bedside drawer, not on a keyring with other common keys, and certainly not hidden in plain sight. Consider a separate, secure location, perhaps a small lockbox of its own, or a designated safe deposit

box. For quick-access defensive firearms, the key should be readily accessible to the authorized user but not to anyone else.

4. **Habit Formation:** For any firearm that is subject to a locking device, the habit of removing the lock should be ingrained as the *very first* action upon handling the firearm. This applies to practice, cleaning, maintenance, and especially in a self-defense scenario. This habit formation is critical to avoid delays or dangerous oversights.

5. **Consideration of Firearm Purpose:** The intended use of the firearm should influence the choice of locking device. For a firearm intended for home defense, the speed of access is a critical factor. While security is paramount, a lock that takes an inordinate amount of time to disengage might be impractical and could compromise a defensive capability. In such cases, a balance must be struck, perhaps opting for a quick-access safe in conjunction with a device that can be swiftly removed. For firearms that are purely for sport or collection and not intended for immediate defensive use, more robust or time-consuming locking mechanisms might be appropriate.

6. **Regular Inspection:** Periodically inspect the locking device for wear and tear.

The coating on cables can degrade, locking mechanisms can become stiff, and keys can bend or break. A worn-out lock is a compromised lock.

7. **Supplement, Not Replace:** Reiterate that these devices are best viewed as supplementary. They significantly enhance security but should not be considered a replacement for a quality firearm safe, particularly for long-term storage or when the highest level of protection against theft and environmental factors is required.

The use of trigger locks, cable locks, and pistol grip locks represents a practical and often necessary component of responsible firearm ownership. They provide accessible and affordable means to enhance security, prevent accidents, and deter unauthorized access. By understanding their advantages, limitations, and by adhering to best practices in their selection and use, firearm owners can create a more secure environment for their families and communities, while maintaining appropriate access to their firearms when lawfully and responsibly needed. These devices are not merely accessories; they are vital tools in the continuum of firearm safety and security.

Ammunition Storage Safety and Environmental Control

The integrity and safety of stored firearms are paramount, but this responsibility extends critically to the ammunition itself. Ammunition, by its very nature, is designed to store and release energy, and as such, requires careful consideration in its storage to prevent accidents, maintain its efficacy, and ensure the overall security of a firearm system. Improperly stored ammunition can degrade over time, leading to misfires or malfunctions, rendering firearms unreliable. More critically, it can present a significant safety hazard if stored in environments that compromise its stability or if it is easily accessible to unauthorized individuals, particularly children. Therefore, a comprehensive approach to firearm security must encompass a detailed strategy for ammunition storage, focusing on both environmental control and security measures.

The cornerstone of safe ammunition storage is maintaining an environment that is both cool and dry. Extreme temperatures and humidity are the primary enemies of gunpowder and primers. High humidity can lead to the absorption of moisture by the propellant, causing it to degrade and become less potent, or in some cases, rendering it entirely inert. This moisture ingress can manifest as corrosion on the casing or, more insidiously, as chemical breakdown within the propellant itself.

Conversely, excessive heat can accelerate the chemical reactions within the ammunition, potentially leading to pressure build-up, premature ignition, or degradation of the propellant and primer compounds. This is why basements, attics, and garages, which often experience significant temperature fluctuations and higher humidity levels, are generally considered suboptimal storage locations unless actively climate-controlled. The ideal storage environment mimics the conditions recommended for long-term preservation of sensitive materials: a stable, moderate temperature range, typically between 50 and 70 degrees Fahrenheit (10 to 21 degrees Celsius), and a low relative humidity, ideally below 50 percent.

To achieve these conditions, specialized storage containers play a crucial role. While ammunition can be kept in its original factory packaging, these boxes are often flimsy and not designed for long-term protection against environmental factors or robust security. Investing in dedicated ammunition storage containers is a wise precaution. These containers are typically constructed from durable plastic or metal and are designed to be airtight and watertight. Many feature robust sealing mechanisms, such as O-rings, which effectively prevent the ingress of moisture and air. Some containers are also lined with desiccant materials or have provisions for adding them, which actively absorb any residual moisture within the container, further ensuring a dry environment. Metal ammunition cans, often referred to as "ammo cans," are a popular and effective choice. They are typically made of steel, are powder-coated for corrosion resistance, and feature a hinged lid with a gasket seal. Their robust construction offers a degree of physical security in addition to environmental protection.

The principle of separation between firearms and ammunition, when feasible and appropriate, is another critical aspect of a layered security strategy. While it is common for defensive firearms to be stored loaded or with readily accessible ammunition for immediate deployment, this should be a deliberate and calculated decision based on the specific needs and risks of the household. For general storage, particularly for firearms not intended for immediate defense or for ammunition stored in bulk, keeping them in separate secure locations can add an extra layer of security. For example, firearms might be stored in a locked safe, while ammunition could be stored in a separate, smaller, locked container or safe in a different location. This separation means that even if one secure location is compromised, the other remains secure, preventing a potential perpetrator from acquiring both the firearm and its means of function simultaneously.

This is particularly relevant in households with children or where there is a higher risk of opportunistic theft.

The risks associated with improperly stored ammunition are multifaceted. Degraded ammunition is a primary concern for firearm functionality. Propellants that have absorbed moisture can burn inconsistently or not at all, leading to "duds" or squibs, where the projectile lodges in the barrel, creating a dangerous obstruction. This obstruction, if not detected before a subsequent round is fired, can cause catastrophic failure of the firearm. Primers can also degrade, becoming less sensitive and requiring a stronger firing pin strike to ignite. This can lead to failures to fire, which, in a defensive scenario, can be critically detrimental. Beyond functionality, the safety risks are significant. Ammunition stored in fluctuating temperatures or high humidity can become unstable. While accidental ignition of a single round of ammunition due to environmental factors alone is extremely rare, the accumulation of heat in a confined space containing large quantities of ammunition could, under extreme circumstances, lead to a sympathetic detonation, though this is a highly improbable event under normal storage conditions. However, the primary risk remains the potential for unauthorized access.

Ammunition, like firearms, must be secured against access by individuals who are not authorized or trained to handle it, most notably children.

When considering bulk storage of ammunition, especially for collectors or those who purchase in large quantities, the principles of environmental control and security become even more pronounced. Large quantities of ammunition generate more heat and are more susceptible to humidity issues if not properly contained. For long-term storage of thousands of rounds, investing in climate-controlled storage solutions, such as a dedicated, dehumidified safe or a separate storage room with environmental controls, becomes advisable. In such scenarios, the ammunition should be stored in robust, sealed containers, and ideally, individual boxes or trays within these containers should also be protected from moisture. The use of multiple layers of protection, such as placing factory boxes within sealed plastic bags, and then placing those into a larger, airtight ammo can or safe, provides a high degree of assurance against environmental degradation.

The physical security of ammunition storage also warrants careful attention. While a firearm safe provides excellent security for both firearms and ammunition, smaller quantities of ammunition may be adequately secured in dedicated, locked ammunition safes or lockboxes. These are often smaller, more compact safes designed specifically for ammunition, but they can also serve to store other valuables. They are typically made of steel and feature a robust locking mechanism, often a key lock or a digital keypad. The key principle here is that the ammunition should be stored in a manner that is inaccessible to unauthorized individuals. If the primary firearm safe is not readily accessible, or if the firearm is stored separately, then the ammunition must be secured in a commensurate fashion. The goal is to ensure that even if unauthorized individuals gain access to a general storage area, the ammunition itself remains protected and inaccessible.

It is also prudent to consider the lifespan of ammunition. While modern ammunition, when stored correctly, can remain viable for many years, even decades, it is not immortal. Propellants and primers will eventually degrade, and metallic components can corrode. For ammunition that is being stored for extended periods, it is good practice to periodically inspect it. This inspection should involve checking for any signs of corrosion on the casing, particularly around the primer and the neck of the casing. Signs of bulging or deformation of the casing can indicate pressure issues. A visual inspection of the powder through the case mouth, if possible, can sometimes reveal caking or discoloration, though this is not always a definitive indicator of degradation. Ammunition that shows significant signs of corrosion, degradation, or damage should be safely disposed of, rather than risking its use. Reputable firearm dealers or shooting ranges often have procedures for the safe disposal of old or degraded ammunition.

When discussing the separation of firearms and ammunition, it is crucial to acknowledge that this is not always practical or desirable, particularly in the context of home defense. A loaded firearm stored in a quick-access safe or mounted securely for immediate deployment would logically have its ammunition stored either within the firearm itself, in a magazine inserted into the firearm, or in a readily accessible, secured location immediately adjacent to the firearm. In such scenarios, the focus shifts to the security of the firearm itself and the responsible management of access to both the firearm and its ammunition. The principle here is that the authorized user must have swift, unimpeded access, while unauthorized individuals must be effectively prevented from accessing either. This is where the judicious use of quick-access safes, biometric safes, or other rapidly deployable security solutions becomes essential.

Furthermore, the type of ammunition being stored can also influence storage practices.

For example, ammunition with specialized propellants or primers, such as those used in some high-performance rounds or certain hunting loads, may have specific storage recommendations from the manufacturer. While most standard sporting ammunition can be stored under the general principles outlined above, it is always wise to consult the manufacturer's guidelines if available, especially for less common types of ammunition.

In essence, the secure storage of ammunition is an integral part of responsible firearm ownership, no less critical than the secure storage of the firearms themselves. It requires a proactive approach that prioritizes both environmental control and physical security. By understanding the vulnerabilities of ammunition to environmental factors like heat and humidity, and by employing appropriate storage containers and locations, owners can ensure the longevity and reliability of their ammunition. Simultaneously, by implementing security measures that prevent unauthorized access, particularly by children, owners can mitigate the significant risks associated with unsecured ammunition. Whether stored in bulk for sporting purposes or as part of a home defense plan, ammunition demands the same level of diligence and care as the firearms it serves, forming a critical, often overlooked, component of overall firearm safety and security.

Environmental Considerations for Firearm Preservation

The integrity of any firearm, from its most basic function to its long-term viability, is intrinsically linked to its environment. Firearms are intricate assemblies of metal parts, and metal, as many a homeowner has discovered, is remarkably susceptible to the insidious creep of rust and corrosion when exposed to moisture and humidity. This is not merely an aesthetic concern; rust can impede the smooth operation of crucial moving parts, seize up actions, and, in severe cases, compromise the structural integrity of the firearm. Therefore, a proactive and informed approach to environmental protection is not an optional extra for the responsible firearm owner; it is a fundamental tenet of ownership, ensuring both the reliability of the tool and the safety of its user.

Understanding the primary adversary – moisture – is the first step in effective environmental protection. Water, in its liquid or vaporous form, is the catalyst for the electrochemical process that leads to rust, a form of iron oxide. High humidity, even without visible water droplets, provides a constant source of this moisture. Temperature fluctuations exacerbate the problem. When warm, humid air comes into contact with a cooler metal surface, condensation occurs. This creates microscopic beads of water that sit on the metal, initiating the rusting process. Think of a cold soda can on a humid summer day; the condensation that forms on the outside is a tangible demonstration of this principle at work. A firearm, especially one that has been handled, will have microscopic oils and perspiration from the skin, which, when combined with moisture, can accelerate corrosion. This is why frequent handling of firearms without proper cleaning and re-oiling is a common precursor to rust formation, particularly in humid climates or during warmer months.

The most fundamental technique for combating moisture is the diligent application of appropriate lubricants and protectants. Firearm oils and cleaning solvents are formulated not just to remove fouling but also to leave a protective film on metal surfaces. This film acts as a barrier, preventing direct contact between the metal and atmospheric moisture. When it comes to oiling, a common mistake is either too little or too much. Too little oil leaves parts vulnerable, while an excessive amount can attract dust and debris, creating an abrasive paste that can actually damage the firearm over time. The key is a thin, even coat applied to all metal surfaces, paying particular attention to areas that are more prone to rust, such as the bore, the exterior of the barrel, the slide, and any exposed metal components. After firing, immediate cleaning and re-oiling are paramount. Residue from gunpowder and primers is often acidic and highly corrosive, and its presence on metal surfaces, combined with residual moisture from firing, creates a perfect storm for rust. A thorough cleaning to remove all fouling, followed by a light application of preservative oil, is the standard practice for post-shooting maintenance.

Beyond basic oiling, specialized products and accessories offer enhanced protection. Desiccant packs, those small, unassuming pouches often found in new shoe boxes or electronics packaging, are invaluable tools for firearm preservation. These packs contain materials like silica gel that actively absorb moisture from the surrounding air. Placing a few desiccant packs within a gun safe, a storage case, or even a sealed plastic bag with a firearm can significantly lower the humidity in that confined space. It is crucial, however, to understand that desiccant packs have a finite capacity and will eventually become saturated. Therefore, they need to be periodically "recharged" or replaced. Recharging typically involves drying them out, often by baking them in a low oven, which drives off the absorbed moisture, restoring their absorbent properties. Many high-quality storage containers and gun safes come equipped with built-in desiccant systems or have designated areas for them.

Another highly effective, yet simple, protective measure is the use of gun socks. These are typically made of a soft, lint-free fabric treated with silicone. When a firearm is placed inside a gun sock, the silicone treatment imparts a protective coating onto the metal surfaces. This provides an additional layer of defense against scratches and, crucially, against moisture. Gun socks are particularly useful for transporting firearms or for storing them within a larger case or safe, adding an extra barrier between the firearm and potential environmental hazards. They are an economical and highly practical addition to any firearm owner's arsenal of protective measures.

The storage location itself plays a pivotal role in environmental protection. As discussed previously regarding ammunition, areas prone to extreme temperature fluctuations and high humidity – such as basements, attics, and garages – are generally poor choices for long-term firearm storage, unless actively climate-controlled. Basements can be damp, attics can become ovens in the summer and freezers in the winter, and garages often share these undesirable characteristics. A controlled environment, where temperature and humidity are kept within a stable, moderate range, is ideal.

This is where a dedicated gun safe or a climate-controlled storage unit becomes a significant investment for serious firearm owners. Modern gun safes, especially higher-end models, often incorporate features like internal lighting and ventilation, and some even have options for integrated dehumidifiers or hygrometers to monitor and regulate humidity levels.

For those who do not have access to a climate-controlled safe or storage room, there are still effective strategies. If storing firearms in a more general-purpose safe, consider placing a small, battery-operated digital hygrometer inside. This inexpensive device will allow you to monitor the humidity levels within the safe. If the humidity consistently rises above 50%, it indicates that additional desiccant or a more active dehumidification solution may be necessary. Small, plug-in electric dehumidifiers designed for safes are also available and can be very effective in maintaining low humidity levels. These devices typically use a heating element to drive off moisture, which is then often vented or collected.

The material and construction of storage containers also matter. While basic plastic gun cases offer some protection against dust and minor impacts, they are generally not airtight or watertight and offer minimal protection against humidity.

For longer-term storage or for firearms of significant value, investing in a more robust, sealed container is advisable. Many high-quality hard gun cases feature O-ring seals around the lid, providing excellent protection against moisture and dust ingress. These are particularly useful for firearms that might be stored in less-than-ideal environments or for those that are transported frequently. Metal ammunition cans, as mentioned earlier, are also excellent for storing smaller firearms or accessories, offering a high degree of environmental protection when sealed properly.

The process of cleaning and oiling should also consider the specific firearm. Different materials and finishes require slightly different approaches. For example, firearms with blued finishes are more susceptible to rust than those with stainless steel or polymer components. While stainless steel is more corrosion-resistant, it is not rust-proof, and prolonged exposure to moisture can still lead to surface rust, especially in pitted areas or around roll marks. Polymer frames are largely immune to rust, but the internal metal components still require diligent care. For firearms with engraved metal components or intricate checkering, it can be challenging to ensure that oil reaches every nook and cranny. Specialized cleaning brushes, such as brass or nylon bore brushes and small detail brushes, can be very helpful in reaching these areas. Some firearm owners also use firearm waxes, which can provide a slightly more durable protective layer than standard oils, especially for firearms that might be stored for extended periods without regular inspection. However, it is crucial to use waxes specifically designed for firearms, as other types of waxes can be too heavy, attract dirt, or even react negatively with certain finishes.

When storing firearms that have been exposed to adverse conditions, such as rain or high humidity, an immediate and thorough cleaning is essential. Do not simply wipe down the exterior. Field strip the firearm (disassemble it according to the manufacturer's instructions) and clean every part, paying close attention to the bore, the action, and any areas where moisture could have pooled. Use a good quality firearm cleaner to remove all fouling and old oil, then dry each part thoroughly with a clean, lint-free cloth. Once completely dry, reassemble the firearm and apply a thin, even coat of preservative oil to all metal surfaces. If the firearm has been submerged in water, even fresh water, it is advisable to clean and lubricate it as soon as possible to prevent immediate rust formation. Saltwater exposure is far more corrosive and requires an even more immediate and rigorous cleaning process.

The practice of storing firearms is not static; it requires ongoing attention and periodic checks. Even in a controlled environment, humidity levels can fluctuate, and desiccant packs can become saturated. Therefore, it is good practice to periodically inspect your stored firearms. This inspection should include checking for any signs of rust, corrosion, or degradation of finishes. It's also an opportunity to ensure that the protective coatings are still intact and to reapply oil or other protectants as needed. This regular maintenance is not just about preserving the firearm's value; it's about ensuring its reliability and safety. A rusted-out firing pin or a corroded barrel can lead to dangerous malfunctions.

Consider the material of the storage container itself. While metal gun safes offer excellent security, they can sometimes be susceptible to condensation if they are not properly managed or if they are placed in an unconditioned space. If you notice any condensation forming on the inside walls of your safe, it indicates a humidity problem that needs to be addressed immediately. This might involve increasing the capacity of your desiccant, using an electric dehumidifier, or improving the ventilation of the safe. Some safe manufacturers offer specific advice on managing humidity within their products, and it's always wise to consult these recommendations.

The interaction between different materials within a storage environment also warrants consideration. For instance, storing firearms directly next to other metal objects, especially those that might be prone to rust themselves, could potentially create a galvanic corrosion situation, where one metal corrodes preferentially. It's generally best to keep firearms separated from other potentially corrosive items and to use protective sleeves or soft cloths to prevent metal-on-metal contact. Similarly, some foam padding materials used in older gun cases can degrade over time and release chemicals that can damage firearm finishes. Modern, high-quality gun cases and safe interiors typically use inert materials, but it's always a good practice to be aware of the materials your firearms are in contact with.

In summary, protecting firearms from environmental damage, primarily rust and corrosion, is an ongoing process that demands vigilance and the application of practical techniques. From the fundamental importance of proper cleaning and lubrication to the strategic use of desiccants and gun socks, each step contributes to the preservation of the firearm. Choosing an appropriate storage location, ideally climate-controlled, and utilizing effective storage containers further fortifies the firearm against the elements. Regular inspections and maintenance ensure that these protective measures remain effective, guaranteeing the reliability, longevity, and safety of your firearms, which is an indispensable component of responsible firearm ownership.

Chapter 4:

Mastering the Fundamentals of Marksmanship

The Pillars of Accuracy Primary Marksmanship Fundamentals

The journey from aiming to impact is a complex interplay of precise physical actions and mental focus. For the firearm to achieve its intended purpose – to deliver a projectile accurately to a designated point – a series of fundamental actions must be performed with meticulous consistency. These actions, often referred to as the pillars of accuracy, form the bedrock of all proficient marksmanship. Without a firm grasp of these principles, any attempt at precision shooting will be akin to building a house on shifting sand. We are not simply pointing and pulling a trigger; we are engaging in a deliberate, controlled sequence designed to translate intention into physical reality with unwavering fidelity. Mastering these fundamentals is not a singular event but a continuous process of refinement, a commitment to understanding the "why" behind each action, and the dedication to executing them with an almost unconscious competence. Each element, from the initial footing to the final release of the shot, contributes to the overall stability and accuracy of the firearm system.

Let us begin with the foundation upon which all shooting stability rests: the stance. Your stance is your connection to the earth, the point from which all subsequent actions emanate. A stable platform is paramount. Imagine trying to paint a masterpiece while standing on a rolling ship; your ability to control the brush, and therefore the outcome of your strokes, would be severely compromised. The same principle applies to marksmanship. A shooter must adopt a posture that provides a solid, balanced base, capable of absorbing the recoil of the firearm without undue disturbance. There are several recognized stances, but they all share common principles. For a right-handed shooter, this typically involves placing the feet shoulder-width apart or slightly wider, with the non-dominant foot slightly forward. This creates a natural lean into the target, distributing weight effectively. The knees should be slightly bent, not locked, allowing for a relaxed yet firm posture. The torso should be upright but not rigid, angled slightly towards the target. The goal is to create a balanced equilibrium, allowing the shooter to remain steady while engaging the trigger and managing recoil. The exact configuration can be personalized to a degree, based on individual body mechanics and comfort, but the underlying principle of a stable, balanced platform remains non-negotiable. A shooter who is constantly shifting their weight or struggling to maintain balance will find their shots drifting unpredictably. Practicing dry fire exercises, focusing solely on achieving and holding a perfect stance, can significantly ingrain this crucial element. One should feel rooted, yet agile, ready to absorb the shot and transition to the next if necessary.

Following the stance, we move to the critical interface between the shooter and the firearm: the grip. The grip is how you hold the weapon, and its effectiveness directly influences your ability to control the firearm's movement, especially under recoil. A proper grip ensures that the firearm is held securely enough to prevent it from moving excessively during the shot, but not so tightly that it induces tension and tremor. Tension is the enemy of accuracy. For a semi-automatic pistol, the grip is typically a two-handed affair, maximizing control and stability. The dominant hand forms the primary grip, with the thumb resting along the side of the frame, avoiding contact with the slide or any moving parts. The web of the shooting hand, the area between the thumb and index finger, should be positioned high on the backstrap of the pistol to facilitate better control and a more direct line of recoil management. The support hand then wraps around the dominant hand, filling any gaps and providing additional contact and pressure. The fingers of the support hand should interlock or overlap with the fingers of the shooting hand to create a unified, solid grip. For a rifle, the grip is equally important, albeit different in execution. The firing hand grasps the pistol grip, similar to a handgun, with a high thumb position. The support hand, often referred to as the "handguard grip" or "CLS grip," is placed forward on the handguard, providing stability and control. The exact position varies based on rifle configuration and shooter preference, but the goal is to create a solid point of contact that helps manage muzzle rise and aids in bringing the rifle back on target for subsequent shots. In all cases, the pressure applied should be firm but not death-like. Think of holding a delicate bird – you want to hold it securely enough that it cannot escape, but too much pressure will crush it. The same applies to the firearm. Over-gripping introduces unnecessary tension into the arms and shoulders, which can translate into flinching or jerking the trigger. This learned behavior, often called "death grip," is a common impediment to accuracy. Experimentation with varying grip pressure during dry fire can help identify the optimal balance between security and relaxation. The goal is a consistent grip, shot after shot, that allows for minimal disturbance of the firearm's aim.

With the firearm held securely, the focus shifts to the front sight. This is where the concept of sight alignment, the first of the two critical "sight" fundamentals, comes into play.

Sight alignment refers to the relationship between the front sight and the rear sight. When looking down at the sights, the goal is to position the front sight

within the rear sight so that they appear centered and at the same height. Imagine two dark tunnels, one slightly larger than the other. You want the smaller tunnel (the front sight) to be perfectly centered within the larger tunnel (the rear sight), and for the tops of both tunnels to be level. If the front sight is too high, too low, or off-center within the rear sight, the bullet will not travel to where you are aiming. This alignment is achieved by making *adjustments with the firearm*, not by moving your head or eyes excessively. The shooter's eye should be positioned at a consistent distance from the rear sight, allowing for a clear, focused view of the front sight. A common error is to focus on the rear sight, or to try and get both front and rear sights into sharp focus simultaneously. The human eye can only clearly focus on one plane at a time. Therefore, the front sight must be the focal point. The rear sight will appear slightly blurred, and the target will be significantly blurred, but the front sight must be perfectly aligned within the rear sight. This precise positioning of the front sight within the rear sight aperture is the essence of sight alignment.

Once the front sight is correctly aligned within the rear sight, the next step is to introduce the target and create what is known as the sight picture. Sight picture is the mental image created by the alignment of the sights and the point of aim on the target. It is the complete visual representation that the shooter intends to achieve before pressing the trigger. With the front sight perfectly centered and level in the rear sight, the shooter then superimposes this aligned sight system onto the desired point of impact on the target. The front sight should be placed slightly *below* the absolute center of the target, assuming a standard black bullseye on a lighter background. This creates a clear visual reference, allowing the shooter to see the precise spot they intend to hit. Imagine holding a clock face up to your eye; if you want to hit the very center of the clock, you would place the tip of your aligned sights at the 6 o'clock position on the target. This ensures that the front sight, which is the most critical element for accuracy, is not obscured by the target itself. The target will appear blurred, as the eye is focused on the front sight, but this blur is acceptable and, in fact, necessary for consistent accuracy. The blur of the target indicates that the front sight is in sharp focus, and therefore correctly aligned. The shooter must develop the discipline to accept this blur and trust the sight alignment they have achieved. A sight picture is achieved when the aligned sights are placed on the precise point of the target that you intend to hit, with the front sight appearing in sharp focus and correctly positioned relative to the rear sight.

The culmination of the preparatory stages – stance, grip, sight alignment, and sight picture – is the execution of trigger control. This is arguably the most critical and often the most challenging fundamental to master. Trigger control is the ability to manipulate the trigger to discharge the firearm without disturbing the sight picture. It is the deliberate and controlled application of pressure that breaks the shot cleanly. A smooth, consistent trigger press is paramount. It should be initiated by the pad of the index finger, applied straight to the rear, and increased progressively until the shot breaks. The pressure should be applied so that the movement of the trigger is masked by the natural movement of the sights and the unavoidable movement of the firearm during discharge. Ideally, the shot should surprise the shooter. This means that the trigger press was so smooth and consistent that the moment the firearm fired, the shooter was not anticipating it and therefore did not flinch or react inappropriately. A common mistake is "milking" the trigger, or jerking it backward, which causes the muzzle to dip or rise just as the shot is fired, predictably throwing the projectile off target. Another error is anticipating the recoil, tensing up in preparation for the bang, which also leads to disruptive movement. Effective trigger control requires a conscious effort to relax the muscles in the hand and arm, allowing for a smooth, deliberate press. The index finger should be placed on the trigger so that the first joint, or the pad of the finger, is in contact. The amount of finger on the trigger can vary based on the trigger design and shooter preference, but the key is consistency and control. As pressure is applied, the shooter should remain focused on the front sight and the desired point of aim. When the trigger breaks, the shooter should maintain their sight picture and follow-through.

This concept of follow-through is the final, yet essential, element in the sequence of accurate shooting. Follow-through is the continuation of all the shooting actions after the projectile has left the barrel. It means maintaining your stance, grip, sight picture, and trigger finger position even after the shot has been fired. Many shooters relax immediately after the shot, or cease to focus on their sights, often out of anticipation of the recoil or simply because the immediate task of firing the shot is complete. However, this is a critical mistake. The firearm is still in motion immediately after the shot breaks. The recoil is still developing, and any disturbance during this critical period can affect the flight of the bullet. A proper follow-through ensures that the firearm's trajectory is not unduly influenced by the shooter's reaction to the shot. Imagine a golfer who stops their swing the moment the club strikes the ball. The resulting shot would likely be erratic. Similarly, a shooter who ceases to actively manage their shooting platform and sight alignment after the shot is compromising their accuracy. Maintaining the grip, keeping the sights aligned on the target, and holding the trigger to the rear until the recoil has subsided and the sights have settled back onto the target are all hallmarks of good follow-through. This allows the shooter to observe the shot's impact, gather critical feedback for future shots, and prepare for a follow-up shot if necessary, ensuring that the process of accurate shooting is continuous and controlled, rather than a series of isolated events. By diligently practicing and integrating these eight fundamental elements – stance, grip, sight alignment, sight picture, trigger control, and follow-through – shooters build a robust and repeatable system for delivering accurate shots. Each pillar is indispensable, and neglecting any one of them will inevitably lead to diminished accuracy. It is through the disciplined and consistent application of these principles that true marksmanship is achieved.

Stance The Stable Platform for Precision

The foundation of any proficient shooting endeavor lies in establishing a stable platform. This isn't merely about standing still; it's about creating a controlled, balanced posture that allows for consistent application of all subsequent shooting skills.

Your stance is your anchor, the point from which all controlled movements – the trigger press, the management of recoil, and any necessary transitions – will originate. Without a stable stance, the finer points of marksmanship become exercises in futility, as any minor imbalance will translate into significant deviations downrange. Think of an architect designing a building; the strongest structures begin with a robust and well-engineered foundation. Similarly, for a shooter, the stance is that foundational element, designed to minimize unwanted movement and maximize control over the firearm.

The biomechanics of a stable stance are rooted in distributing your weight effectively and creating a low center of gravity. This minimizes the body's natural sway and provides a solid base to absorb the energetic forces generated by a firearm's discharge. While various recognized stances exist, they all adhere to fundamental principles of balance, stability, and biomechanical efficiency. We will explore two of the most widely adopted and effective stances: the Isosceles and the Modified Weaver. Each offers unique advantages, and understanding their mechanics will empower you to choose or adapt a stance that best suits your physiology and shooting discipline. The goal is not to find a "one size fits all" solution, but to understand the principles so you can achieve a personalized, stable platform.

The Isosceles stance, named for the two symmetrical muscles of the thigh, presents a balanced and forward-facing posture. In this stance, the shooter positions their feet roughly shoulder-width apart, with their body squared up towards the target. Both arms are extended towards the firearm, forming a triangular or "isosceles" shape with the shooter's body and the firearm. The feet are typically positioned parallel to each other, or with the support-side foot slightly back for a more natural feel. Weight is distributed evenly between both feet, with a slight forward bias. The knees are kept unlocked and slightly bent, allowing for a natural flex and the ability to absorb recoil through subtle adjustments in the legs and hips. The upper body is kept upright but not rigid, with the torso angled slightly forward, creating a natural lean into the target. This forward lean is crucial for managing recoil and maintaining an integrated platform. The head is held naturally, aligned with the spine, and the shooter looks through the sights.

The primary advantage of the Isosceles stance is its inherent stability and excellent recoil management. By presenting a broad base and extending both arms, the shooter creates a strong connection to the firearm. The forward lean and slight bend in the knees allow the shooter's body to act as a shock absorber, dissipating the energy of the recoil in a controlled manner. This is particularly beneficial for managing muzzle rise, allowing for faster and more accurate follow-up shots. Furthermore, the symmetrical nature of the stance makes it adaptable for both right and left-handed shooters, and it's a highly effective platform for a wide range of firearms, from handguns to rifles. In a practical sense, imagine yourself as a spring. When the shot is fired, your bent knees and forward lean allow you to compress slightly, absorbing the jolt, and then rebound smoothly, bringing the sights back to the target. The key to mastering the Isosceles stance lies in finding that sweet spot of balanced weight distribution and a relaxed, yet firm, posture. Avoid locking your knees, as this renders you rigid and unable to absorb recoil effectively. Conversely, avoid excessive bending, which can lead to fatigue and instability.

Transitioning to the Modified Weaver stance, we encounter a configuration that offers a slightly different approach to stability, often favored for its power and ability to absorb recoil with a strong grip. Developed by the legendary firearms instructor Jack Weaver, this stance has been adapted and modified over the years, hence the "modified" designation. In this stance, the shooter positions their feet at a slight angle, with the non-dominant foot forward.

For a right-handed shooter, the left foot would be forward, and for a left-handed shooter, the right foot would be forward. The feet are typically placed about shoulder-width apart or slightly wider, creating a stable base. The body is turned slightly away from the target, so the shooting shoulder is more forward. The dominant arm is slightly bent at the elbow, while the non-dominant arm is extended more, but still with a slight bend. The key element of the Modified Weaver is the opposing forces generated by the hands and arms. The shooting hand grips the firearm firmly, while the support hand pushes forward. This opposing pressure, along with the slight bend in the knees and the forward lean of the torso, creates a stable platform that effectively counteracts recoil.

The Modified Weaver stance excels in its ability to manage recoil due to the way the opposing forces of the arms are utilized. The forward pressure from the support hand, combined with the recoil impulse from the firearm, helps to drive the firearm back into the shooter's shoulder or hand in a controlled manner. This can lead to less muzzle flip and a more stable shooting platform, especially for larger caliber firearms or when shooting rapidly. The slight turn of the body also contributes to a more natural shooting posture for some individuals, and the forward foot placement can aid in recoil absorption through the legs.

However, it's important to note that this stance can sometimes lead to a more pronounced recoil into the shoulder for those who aren't effectively engaging their support hand's pushing force. The modification often seen today involves a more forward placement of the support hand on the handguard of a rifle, or a more extended support arm on a pistol, emphasizing the creation of a strong, unified shooting platform. As with the Isosceles, proper weight distribution is crucial. The weight should be balanced between the feet, with a slight forward bias to aid in recoil management. The knees should be bent, and the torso angled forward, allowing the body to absorb recoil effectively.

Regardless of the specific stance chosen, several universal principles contribute to a stable and effective shooting platform. Firstly, foot placement is paramount. Your feet should be positioned at a width that provides a stable base, typically around shoulder-width apart or slightly wider. Avoid standing with your feet too close together, as this creates a narrow base susceptible to imbalance, or too far apart, which can lead to fatigue and an inability to shift weight effectively. The angle of your feet relative to the target should allow for a natural and balanced posture. For most shooters, a slight angle, with the non-dominant foot slightly forward, proves most comfortable and biomechanically sound. This allows for a natural lean into the target and facilitates recoil absorption.

Secondly, weight distribution is critical. The majority of your weight should be balanced between your feet, with a slight forward bias. This forward lean helps to absorb recoil and keep the firearm pressing into the target. Avoid leaning too far back, as this will cause the muzzle to rise excessively during recoil. Conversely, leaning too far forward can lead to instability and an unnatural posture. Imagine you are standing on a gently sloping hill, facing downhill. You would naturally lean forward slightly to maintain balance. This is a good analogy for the ideal weight distribution in a shooting stance.

Thirdly, maintaining a relaxed yet firm posture is essential. Locked knees and rigid muscles create tension, which is the enemy of accuracy. Instead, keep your knees slightly bent, allowing them to act as shock absorbers. Your torso should be upright but not stiff, angled slightly towards the target. Your shoulders should be relaxed, and your head held naturally, aligned with your spine. This relaxed posture allows your body to absorb recoil without transmitting excessive movement to the firearm. The "firm" aspect comes from the engagement of your core muscles and the consistent pressure applied through your arms to the firearm, creating a cohesive shooting platform.

Finally, the practice of "pre-firing" or dry fire exercises is invaluable for ingraining a proper stance. Stand in your chosen stance, and without a firearm, focus on achieving a balanced, stable position. Hold this position for an extended period, paying attention to any areas of tension or imbalance. Then, introduce the firearm (unloaded, of course) and practice assuming your stance, ensuring that your grip and sight alignment are achieved from this stable base. Repeat this process many times. The goal is to make the act of assuming a proper stance an almost automatic, unconscious action, so that when you are under the stress of a live-fire situation, your body instinctively defaults to a stable and balanced platform. This consistent application of fundamental principles, whether through dry fire or live fire, will build muscle memory and ensure that your stance becomes a reliable foundation for all your shooting skills. Remember, your stance is your connection to the ground, and a strong connection is the first step towards accurate shooting.

Grip Control and Consistency

The grip, the point of contact between the shooter and the firearm, is arguably the most critical element in achieving consistent accuracy and effective control. It is the conduit through which all the shooter's intentions are translated into the firearm's action, and conversely, the mechanism by which the firearm's forces are managed. A solid, repeatable grip ensures that the firearm remains stable in the face of recoil, allows for precise trigger manipulation, and enables rapid, accurate follow-up shots.

Without a proper grip, even the most stable stance and perfect sight alignment can be rendered ineffective by the dynamic forces of firing. Think of it as the handshake you offer the firearm; it needs to be firm, confident, and consistent every single time. This isn't about brute strength; it's about applying the correct amount of pressure in the right places to create a unified shooting platform.

For most semi-automatic pistols, the dominant hand forms the core of the grip. The web of skin between your thumb and index finger should be placed as high as possible on the backstrap of the pistol, without interfering with the slide's movement. This high grip allows you to get your hand closer to the bore axis, which significantly reduces the leverage that recoil has on the firearm, thereby minimizing muzzle rise. Your dominant thumb should be extended forward, generally resting on the frame or along the side of the firearm, depending on your preference and the firearm's design. This thumb position can serve to brace against the frame or even provide a contact point for the support hand. The index finger should remain relaxed and off the trigger until you are ready to engage it. The remaining three fingers of your dominant hand wrap around the grip, applying consistent pressure.

The role of the support hand is equally crucial in a two-handed pistol grip. It acts to reinforce the dominant hand, further stabilizing the firearm and aiding in recoil management. The support hand should encompass the dominant hand completely, with the palm filling the gaps. Ideally, the thumb of the support hand should lie along the same plane as the dominant hand's thumb, or slightly forward, again depending on the shooter's anatomy and the firearm. The fingers of the support hand should interlock or press firmly against the dominant hand's fingers, creating a single, cohesive unit. The key to a successful two-handed grip is the application of equal and consistent pressure from both hands. Imagine a vise; both jaws are applying pressure, creating a secure hold. Similarly, both your hands should be working together, with the support hand often providing a slight forward pressure to counter the recoil. This opposing pressure helps to keep the firearm from rotating upwards during the shot. This is often referred to as the "push-pull" technique, where the dominant hand pushes forward and the support hand pulls back, or vice versa, creating a rigid structure.

The precise amount of pressure applied is a nuanced aspect of grip. Too little pressure, and the firearm will want to jump and twist in your hand during recoil, making it difficult to reacquire your sights. Too much pressure, however, can lead to tension in your wrists and arms, which will translate into a shaky sight picture and an inconsistent trigger press. The goal is a firm, controlled grip that allows for the firearm to be held securely without causing extraneous muscle tension. A good way to assess your grip pressure is through dry fire practice. Grip the firearm as you normally would, and dry fire. Then, consciously increase the pressure from your support hand. You will likely notice that the sights remain more stable. Now, consciously relax your grip. You'll see the sights wander. The ideal is somewhere in between; a grip firm enough to resist recoil but relaxed enough to allow for fine motor control of the trigger. Many instructors recommend about 70-80% of your maximum grip strength, with the majority of that pressure coming from the support hand. This allows the dominant hand to focus on the precise trigger press.

For rifles, the principles of the two-handed grip are similar, but the application differs due to the firearm's design and the shooter's posture. When shooting a rifle from a standing position, the dominant hand encircles the pistol grip, much like with a handgun, with the web of the hand high on the grip. The support hand plays a crucial role in controlling the forearm and managing recoil. Depending on the rifle type, the support hand might grasp the handguard, the magazine well, or even employ a "c-clamp" grip where the thumb is placed over the top of the handguard and the fingers wrap around the sides. The goal is to create a stable platform that absorbs and manages the rifle's recoil. The support hand's position influences the muzzle rise; a firmer grip and a more forward placement of the support hand can help keep the muzzle down. The support arm should be slightly bent, allowing it to act as a shock absorber. Similar to the handgun, a firm but not tense grip is key. The application of a consistent pressure from both hands helps to channel the recoil directly rearward, minimizing any lateral movement or rotation.

The concept of grip consistency is paramount. Every time you draw a firearm and establish your grip, it needs to be the same. This means the placement of your hands, the pressure applied, and the overall "feel" of the grip should be identical, whether it's your first shot or your hundredth. This consistency is what builds muscle memory and allows for reliable performance. When you draw a pistol, your hands should naturally find their proper positions without conscious thought. This level of automation comes from repetitive, deliberate practice, both on and off the range. Think of it as learning to ride a bicycle; at first, it requires a lot of concentration, but with practice, you no longer think about your balance or how to pedal; your body just does it. The same applies to your grip.

For revolvers, the grip dynamics change due to the absence of a frame-mounted slide and the typical design of the grip. The dominant hand grip is similar in principle to that of a semi-automatic pistol: high on the backstrap, with the thumb positioned to suit the shooter. However, the support hand often plays a more critical role in managing the significant muzzle flip inherent in many revolvers. The most common and effective grip for revolvers is a full two-handed grip, where the support hand fully encompasses the dominant hand. The fingers of the support hand should press firmly against the dominant hand's fingers, and the palm should fill any gaps. The support thumb can be placed along the side of the dominant thumb, or it can be extended forward, resting on the cylinder release or the frame. Some shooters find that extending the support thumb forward, along the top of the dominant thumb, helps to provide additional leverage to control muzzle flip.

The pressure distribution in a revolver grip is also critical. The dominant hand provides the primary hold, but the support hand's ability to "lock out" and press forward against the recoil is what truly tames the beast. The idea is to create a solid block with your hands, so that when the recoil impulse hits, it is directed rearward and absorbed by your arms and body, rather than causing the muzzle to jump erratically. Many shooters find that applying more pressure with the support hand than the dominant hand is beneficial for revolvers, particularly those with larger calibers. This forward pressure from the support hand counteracts the upward thrust of the recoil. It's a delicate balance; too little support hand pressure and you'll experience significant muzzle rise, making follow-up shots slower. Too much tension throughout the grip and you risk flinching or an inconsistent trigger pull.

A common mistake with revolvers is a "death grip" with the dominant hand, leading to tension that transfers to the trigger finger. Conversely, a weak grip with the support hand will lead to instability. The goal is a unified, strong grip where both hands work in concert to control the firearm. For those shooting lighter revolvers or engaging in rapid fire, the ability to manage muzzle flip is paramount. This often requires a strong, proactive support hand that actively pushes against the recoil. The extended support thumb technique is particularly useful here, as it provides a substantial point of contact to resist the firearm's upward tendency.

Ultimately, the "best" grip is the one that allows you, the individual shooter, to achieve consistent accuracy and control with a specific firearm. This requires experimentation and an understanding of the underlying principles. Factors such as hand size, finger length, and even the texture of the grip panels on a firearm can influence what feels and works best. It's essential to experiment with different grip pressures and hand placements during practice, paying close attention to how the firearm behaves during recoil and how it feels in your hands. Dry fire practice, combined with live-fire sessions, will allow you to refine your grip until it becomes an instinctive, reliable extension of your will. Remember, your grip is your direct connection to the firearm; invest the time and effort to make that connection as strong and consistent as possible. It is the foundation upon which all other shooting skills are built.

Trigger Control and the Smooth Break

The transition from a stable grip and proper sight alignment to the actual firing of the shot rests squarely on the shooter's ability to manipulate the trigger effectively. This is where the rubber meets the road, the point at which all prior preparation culminates in the projectile leaving the barrel. Trigger control, more than any other fundamental, is where a shooter's true skill is often revealed, and it is frequently the most difficult aspect to master. It is not merely about pulling the trigger; it is about a controlled, deliberate action that allows the firearm to perform as intended without disturbing the carefully established sight picture.

At its core, proper trigger control is about achieving a smooth, uninterrupted press that culminates in the hammer falling and the firearm discharging. The objective is to press the trigger in such a way that the sights remain perfectly aligned on the target throughout the entire process. This means the trigger press must be initiated *after* the sights are aligned and *maintained* until the shot breaks, and importantly, *after* the shot breaks. The greatest enemy of good trigger control is anticipation – the subconscious desire to influence the outcome of the shot by flinching, jerking, or otherwise reacting to the perceived recoil or the sound of the shot before it happens.

The mechanics of the trigger press itself are deceptively simple, yet require meticulous attention to detail. The primary point of contact with the trigger should be the pad of your index finger, not the tip or the joint. Imagine the trigger as a sensitive lever. You want to apply pressure with the fleshy, broadest part of your fingertip. This provides a larger surface area for consistent pressure application and allows for finer control over the trigger's movement. The exact placement of this pad will vary slightly from person to person, depending on the size of their finger and the shape of the trigger itself. The key is to find a consistent placement that allows for a smooth, straight-line pull.

This pressure should be applied in a slow, steady, and progressive manner. Think of it as a continuous and ever-increasing force that gradually moves the trigger rearward. There should be no sudden jerks or anticipatory movements. Instead, you are building pressure, almost imperceptibly, until the sear releases the hammer or striker, and the shot occurs. This gradual application is crucial because it helps to mask the actual moment of discharge. If the pressure is applied smoothly and steadily, the shooter will not know precisely when the shot will break, thereby minimizing the opportunity for anticipation to cause a flinch.

A common and highly effective technique is to think of the trigger press as a function of the fingertip applying gentle, consistent pressure. As you achieve a perfect sight alignment, you begin to slowly increase the pressure on the trigger. You are not *waiting* for the shot; you are *applying* pressure until the shot happens. This subtle mental shift from "waiting for the shot" to "causing the shot" is fundamental. The finger moves straight back, perpendicular to the bore axis of the firearm, for semi-automatic pistols and rifles. For revolvers, the trigger pull is often curved, so the finger press will follow a slightly arcing path, but the principle of a smooth, straight-line pull relative to the shooter's intent remains the same.

The amount of pressure required varies significantly between different firearms. Some triggers are very light and crisp, requiring only a few pounds of force. Others, particularly double-action revolvers or certain safety-conscious designs, can have much heavier trigger pulls. Regardless of the weight, the technique remains the same: smooth, consistent, and progressive pressure. The goal is to disengage the trigger mechanism without disturbing the sight alignment. This means that as the trigger moves rearward, the sights should remain locked onto the target. Any lateral movement of the finger – pushing left or right – will cause the sights to move off the intended point of impact.

It is imperative to maintain your sight alignment and sight picture *throughout* the entire firing process. This includes the moment the shot breaks and, importantly, for a brief moment *after* the shot. Many shooters are so focused on the action of pulling the trigger that they relax their focus on the sights the instant they feel the recoil or hear the shot. This is a critical error. The firearm is still moving as the bullet is exiting the barrel, and maintaining your sight picture during this phase allows you to observe any subtle movements you might have made and provides feedback for future shots. This post-shot observation is an integral part of understanding how your trigger control affected the shot.

Think of it like this: you're holding a delicate laser pointer perfectly aimed at a distant mark. To keep that laser precisely on target, you can't just aim and then tap a button. You have to maintain that perfect aim as you activate the laser, and for a moment after it's on, to ensure it stays exactly where you want it. The firearm is no different. Your sight alignment is your laser, and the trigger press is your button.

The concept of "surprise break" is fundamental to excellent trigger control. This refers to a trigger pull so smooth and consistent that the shooter has no idea *when* the shot will actually fire. This is achieved by applying steady, increasing pressure without any conscious indication or expectation of the hammer falling. If you can achieve this surprise break, you are far less likely to anticipate the shot and thus far more likely to maintain your sight alignment. It is the ultimate expression of controlled manipulation.

Practicing trigger control can and should be done extensively without live ammunition, through a process known as dry-fire. Dry-firing is an invaluable tool for developing muscle memory and refining the trigger press without the distractions of live ammunition, recoil, and noise. Before engaging in dry-fire, it is crucial to ensure that the firearm is completely unloaded and that no ammunition is present in the immediate vicinity. Treat every firearm as if it were loaded, and always confirm the chamber is empty before beginning any dry-fire exercises.

During dry-fire, you can focus solely on the mechanics of the trigger press. The process typically involves:

1. Achieving a proper grip and stance.

2. Aligning the sights on a designated point (a wall, a safe object, or simply an imaginary target).

3. Initiating a slow, steady, and progressive pressure on the trigger with the pad of your index finger.

4. Observing the front sight. Does it move as you increase pressure? If it moves, you are disturbing your sight alignment.

5. Continuing to build pressure until you hear and feel the trigger mechanism "click" (simulating the shot).

6. Crucially, do *not* release the trigger immediately. Maintain pressure and observe the sights.

7. Then, slowly release the trigger until you hear and feel the reset. As you release, again, observe the sights. Does the sight picture move?

8. Re-engage the trigger, feeling for the reset point. Then, perform another smooth trigger press to the rear.

This meticulous process of engaging and releasing the trigger, observing the sights at every step, is the bedrock of developing excellent trigger control. Many shooters make the mistake of simply pulling the trigger until it clicks and then releasing it. However, observing the sights during the release and reset is equally important. The way the sights behave as the trigger resets can reveal habits or tensions that might be negatively impacting your live-fire performance. For instance, if the sights move as you release the trigger, it suggests you are tensing up or reacting to the simulated shot.

For firearms with a visible hammer, you can manually cock the hammer and then perform the trigger press. For striker-fired firearms, you will need to cycle the slide to reset the striker mechanism between each dry-fire pull. This allows you to practice the full trigger press repeatedly. It is highly recommended to integrate this dry-fire practice into your routine. Even five to ten minutes of deliberate dry-fire practice a few times a week can yield significant improvements in your ability to control the trigger.

Another valuable dry-fire drill involves placing an object on the end of the firearm's barrel, such as a spent casing or a coin. The goal of this drill is to execute a trigger press without causing the casing or coin to fall off.

This drill is a stark visual indicator of any movement in the firearm during the trigger press. If the casing or coin moves, it means the firearm is moving, and thus your sight alignment is being disturbed. This exercise forces you to focus on the smoothness of your trigger pull and the stability of your platform.

When transitioning to live fire, it is essential to remember the principles honed during dry-fire. The sensation of recoil and the sound of the shot can be disorienting, and the temptation to anticipate will be strong. Remind yourself to focus on the fundamentals: grip, stance, sight alignment, and a smooth, progressive trigger press. Imagine you are still dry-firing. Concentrate on building that steady pressure until the shot breaks. Do not be discouraged if your initial shots with live ammunition do not reflect the precision you achieved in dry-fire. This is normal. Consistency and deliberate practice are key to bridging that gap.

It is also important to understand that trigger control is not an isolated skill. It is intrinsically linked to all the other fundamentals of marksmanship. A poor grip will make smooth trigger control difficult, if not impossible. An unsteady stance will cause your sights to wander, making it harder to isolate the trigger press.

Likewise, a poorly executed trigger press can negate perfect grip and sight alignment. Therefore, when troubleshooting accuracy issues, it is crucial to analyze all the fundamentals, not just the trigger. However, when it comes to refining your accuracy, a consistent and smooth trigger press is often the most significant factor.

For some, the challenge with trigger control lies in overcoming a perceived need to "aim and then shoot." This often leads to a conscious effort to time the trigger press precisely with the perfect sight alignment, which invariably results in anticipation. The correct approach is to develop the ability to *maintain* sight alignment *while* applying trigger pressure. This is why the "surprise break" is so highly prized. When you don't know when the shot will break, you are forced to keep your sights aligned for a longer duration, integrating the trigger press into the aiming process rather than treating it as a separate, instantaneous action.

Another aspect to consider is the reset of the trigger. After the shot breaks, and as you are recovering from recoil and reacquiring your sight picture, the trigger will move forward to its reset point. Feeling and understanding this reset is vital for accurate follow-up shots. Some shooters will deliberately release the trigger just enough to feel the reset, and then apply pressure again for the next shot, maintaining a similar smooth build-up of pressure. This "staging" of the trigger can lead to very rapid and accurate follow-up shots, as it shortens the distance the trigger needs to travel for the next discharge. However, for beginners, the primary focus should remain on the initial smooth press to the rear. Mastering the reset comes with further practice and experience.

Finally, be patient with yourself. Trigger control is arguably the most challenging fundamental to master. It requires a high degree of fine motor control, discipline, and the ability to overcome deeply ingrained psychological responses to the act of firing a weapon. Consistent, deliberate practice, both dry-fire and live-fire, is the only way to achieve proficiency. Seek feedback from experienced instructors, and be willing to analyze your own performance objectively. Your ability to control the trigger is the final, crucial step in translating your intent into an accurate shot, and it is a skill that is always worth refining.

Follow Through Completing the Shot Cycle

The shot has broken. The projectile has left the barrel, propelled by the controlled detonation within. But for the marksmanship-minded individual, the process isn't over. In fact, a critical phase, often relegated to an afterthought by the novice, is just beginning: the follow-through. This isn't about dwelling on the past; it's about ensuring the accuracy of the shot just fired and setting the stage for whatever comes next. It's the bridge between a single, isolated event and a consistent, repeatable performance. Without a proper follow-through, even a flawlessly executed trigger press and sight alignment can be undone by the firearm's inherent dynamics of recoil and cycling.

Think of follow-through as maintaining your focus and control *through* the entire event. The moment the shot breaks is not an ending; it's a transition. The firearm is still in motion, the bullet is still traveling down the barrel, and the energy of the discharge is still being absorbed by your body. During this crucial instant and the moments immediately following, a deliberate commitment to maintaining your established shooting platform and sight picture is paramount. This means that the grip you established and refined remains firm, the stance you adopted to absorb recoil stays solid, and your eyes remain locked onto your sights, observing their relationship with the target. The temptation to flinch, to relax, or to simply look away as the recoil hits is immense, but resisting this is the hallmark of disciplined shooting.

The physical act of follow-through involves consciously resisting the natural tendency to react to recoil.

As the shot is fired, the firearm will move. This movement is a combination of the recoil impulse pushing the gun backward and slightly upward, and the internal mechanics of the firearm cycling (if it's a semi-automatic or automatic weapon). Your job is to absorb this energy as effectively as possible through your grip and stance, and to allow your sights to move predictably *with* the firearm, rather than allowing your body to fight the motion in a way that disturbs your sight picture. This means keeping your finger in contact with the trigger as it moves rearward, and even *through* the trigger reset if you are preparing for a follow-up shot. Your focus on the front sight should not waver. You should continue to see the front sight in relation to the rear sight and the target even as the firearm recoils.

This mental discipline is as important as the physical. You must maintain the mental image of the sight alignment you had at the moment of firing. This internal focus helps to keep your body stable and prevents subconscious anticipatory movements that could have influenced the shot even if you didn't consciously perceive it. It's about staying "in the shot" for a beat longer than the actual discharge. Many instructors emphasize continuing to press the trigger *through* the reset point and observing the front sight as it moves.

This creates a continuous feedback loop, showing you exactly how your actions are affecting the firearm's movement.

Consider the analogy of throwing a baseball. A pitcher doesn't just stop their arm motion the instant the ball leaves their hand. The arm continues to move in a fluid, follow-through motion, which contributes to velocity and accuracy. Similarly, in shooting, the follow-through ensures that the momentum of your shooting arm and body is channeled smoothly, rather than being arrested abruptly, which could cause the firearm to move. By maintaining a firm grip and allowing your body to absorb recoil, you are essentially "following through" with the shot.

The duration of this follow-through is important. It's not about staring intently at the target for an extended period after the shot, but rather about maintaining your focus and control for a brief, critical interval. This usually means holding your sight picture and trigger contact until the firearm has settled somewhat after the recoil, and you can clearly see the result of your shot. For semi-automatic firearms, the cycling of the action will also occur during this time. A proper follow-through will ensure that this cycling does not cause excessive muzzle rise or a disruption of your sight picture. You should observe the firearm's movement, learn from it, and be prepared to re-engage the target if necessary.

This preparation for a follow-up shot is a key component of follow-through. If you are shooting in a defensive scenario, or in a timed competition, the ability to make accurate successive shots quickly is crucial. A good follow-through naturally sets you up for this. By maintaining your grip and stance, and keeping your eyes on the sights, you can immediately begin to re-acquire your sight picture as the firearm cycles. You'll feel the trigger reset, and you can then smoothly begin to apply pressure for the next shot, often with minimal adjustment. The muscle memory developed through consistent follow-through practice will enable you to transition from one shot to the next with greater speed and accuracy.

Let's break down the practical application of follow-through.

Firstly, the grip must remain solid. The hand strength you applied during the initial grip should be maintained. You don't want to relax your grip as the recoil hits, as this will allow the firearm to move more erratically and make it harder to control. The grip should be firm enough to absorb recoil but not so tense that it causes unnecessary fatigue or tremor. Think of it as a controlled vise, holding the firearm securely throughout its entire cycle of movement.

Secondly, the stance and body positioning are critical. Your legs should be slightly bent, your core engaged, and your body should be positioned to absorb the recoil effectively. As the shot breaks, your body should absorb the forward impulse of the firearm, allowing it to move in a predictable path. This controlled absorption prevents jerky movements that could disrupt your sight picture. Imagine a controlled spring mechanism; your body is the spring, absorbing and releasing energy in a deliberate manner.

Thirdly, the eyes and mind must remain engaged. This is where the mental aspect of follow-through truly shines. You must consciously keep your eyes focused on the front sight. Even as the recoil pushes the firearm away, your eyes should track the front sight's movement relative to the rear sight. This focus helps to maintain a stable visual reference point. Furthermore, your mind should be processing the information: observing the firearm's movement, feeling the trigger reset, and preparing for the next shot if the situation demands it. This mental engagement prevents a lapse in concentration that can lead to errors.

A common mistake that negates good follow-through is the "peeking" phenomenon. This is when the shooter actively moves their head or eyes to try and see the bullet's impact *before* the firearm has finished its cycle. This is a form of anticipation that directly interferes with the follow-through process. You must let the firearm finish its movement, and trust that your initial sight alignment and trigger press were sufficient. The result of the shot will become apparent shortly thereafter, and it will be far more accurate if you maintain your discipline through the entire process.

Dry-fire practice is an excellent way to isolate and refine the follow-through without the distractions of live ammunition. During dry-fire, you can simulate the shot by pressing the trigger until it "breaks" (the click). After the click, you must consciously maintain your grip, stance, and sight alignment. Observe the front sight and how it moves. Continue to hold the trigger to the rear until you feel and hear the trigger reset. Then, release the trigger slowly, feeling for the reset again, and observing the front sight's movement during the release. This meticulous process allows you to internalize the mechanics of follow-through and identify any involuntary movements you might be making.

One highly effective dry-fire drill for practicing follow-through involves placing a spent casing or a coin on the flat top of the slide or frame of a semi-automatic pistol, or on the barrel of a revolver.

The goal is to execute a trigger press without causing the object to fall. After the "shot" breaks, you must maintain your platform and observe the object. If the object remains in place, it is a strong indicator that your follow-through is solid and you are not introducing unnecessary movement into the firearm. This drill provides immediate, tangible feedback on your ability to control the firearm's dynamics after the shot.

When you transition back to live fire, the principles of follow-through remain identical. The added stimulus of recoil and noise will test your discipline. Remind yourself to stay "in the shot." Maintain your grip, keep your eyes on the sights, and allow your body to absorb the recoil. Resist the urge to flinch or move away from the firearm. Think of it as a continuation of the dry-fire process. Your aim is to make the live-fire experience as similar as possible to the controlled environment of dry-fire, focusing on maintaining your platform throughout the shot's entire cycle.

The benefits of a proper follow-through extend beyond the accuracy of a single shot. It cultivates a consistent shooting rhythm, which is essential for rapid and accurate fire. When you establish a solid follow-through, your body and mind are already in a good position to acquire the sights for the next shot. This reduces the time and effort required for re-acquisition, leading to faster and more accurate follow-up shots.

It creates a smooth, almost seamless transition between firing and preparing for the next engagement.

Furthermore, effective follow-through helps in diagnosing shooting errors. By maintaining your sight picture and grip throughout the recoil, you can more accurately discern what happened during the shot. If your sights move unexpectedly or erratically, it might indicate an issue with your grip, stance, or trigger control that you can then address. Without this diligent observation, it becomes much harder to pinpoint the root cause of inaccuracy. The follow-through provides valuable diagnostic data for self-improvement.

In summary, the follow-through is the often-unsung hero of marksmanship. It is the deliberate commitment to maintaining control, focus, and stability from the moment the shot breaks through the subsequent recoil and cycling of the firearm. It requires both physical discipline – maintaining a firm grip and solid stance – and mental acuity – keeping your eyes on the sights and processing the event. By embracing the follow-through, you not only enhance the accuracy of individual shots but also lay the foundation for a consistent shooting rhythm, faster follow-up shots, and more effective self-diagnosis of shooting errors. It is the final, critical act that transforms a single event into a controlled, repeatable performance, solidifying your mastery over the fundamental principles of marksmanship. Without it, even the most promising shot can be rendered suboptimal by the unmanaged forces unleashed by the firearm itself.

Chapter 5:

Advance Marksmanship and Situational Proficiency

Sight Alignment and Sight Picture Achieving Precision Aim

The journey from basic marksmanship to advanced proficiency is a continuous refinement of fundamental principles. We've touched upon the critical importance of sight alignment and sight picture in the foundational stages, but in this section, we will delve significantly deeper, dissecting these elements with the precision required for consistent, high-level accuracy. Understanding and mastering sight alignment and sight picture is not merely about seeing the sights; it's about understanding the precise, almost surgical, relationship between the firearm, its intended target, and your own perceptual capabilities. This relationship dictates where the projectile will travel, and any deviation, however minute, can translate into a significant miss downrange.

Let's begin by deconstructing what we mean by sight alignment and sight picture. Sight alignment refers to the precise positioning of the front sight within the rear sight. Imagine the rear sight as a gate or a channel, and the front sight as the post that must be correctly placed within that channel. For most modern firearms, particularly handguns and rifles designed for precision, this ideal alignment involves three critical points: the top of the front sight must be perfectly flush with the top of the rear sight, and there must be an equal amount of space, or "light," between the sides of the front sight and the inner walls of the rear sight notch. This equal spacing is crucial. If the space is wider on one side than the other, your front sight will appear visually shifted, and your aim will be equally shifted. The objective is to create a symmetrical visual impression. This perfect alignment ensures that your projectile will travel along the intended line of sight, assuming the target is also correctly placed within this line.

Now, consider sight picture. Sight picture encompasses the alignment of the sights *and* the placement of that aligned sight system on the intended target. It's the complete visual cue you hold in your mind's eye just before and during the trigger press. The correct sight picture means that the perfectly aligned front and rear sights are positioned precisely where you want the bullet to strike on the target. The exact point of aim on the target can vary based on the sights themselves and the shooter's preference or the requirements of the situation. For example, with iron sights that have a square post front sight and a square notch rear sight, the sight picture typically involves aligning the top of the front sight post with the top of the rear sight notch, and then placing the *center* of that front sight post on the desired aiming point of the target. If you're aiming for the center of a bullseye, the front sight post should be centered on that bullseye. If you are aiming for a specific point on an object, the front sight should be placed precisely on that point. The key is the consistent visualization of this complete image – sights aligned, and that alignment precisely placed on the target.

The interplay between these two elements is where precision is born. Inadequate sight alignment, even with a seemingly perfect sight picture, will result in an inaccurate shot. Conversely, perfect sight alignment with an improperly placed sight picture will also lead to a miss. It's a symbiotic relationship; one cannot compensate for a deficiency in the other. The shooter must consciously and consistently achieve both the correct alignment and the correct picture for every shot. This is where practice, repetition, and a keen understanding of visual perception become paramount.

Let's elaborate on the concept of "equal light." When you look at the front sight through the rear sight, you should see a clear, unobstructed view of the front sight post, framed by the rear sight notch. The space on either side of the front sight should appear identical. Imagine a perfectly centered ruler placed within a slightly wider channel.

The ruler is the front sight, and the channel is the rear sight. The space between the ruler's edges and the channel's walls should be the same on both the left and right sides. This equal spacing is not an arbitrary aesthetic; it's a geometrically derived necessity. Because the front sight is closer to your eye than the rear sight, even a slight misalignment of the front sight within the rear sight notch is amplified by the distance to the target. A millimeter of difference at the rear sight can translate to inches of difference at 50 or 100 yards. This is why a consistent, symmetrical gap is so vital.

The quality of your sights themselves plays a role. Front sights come in various widths, from very fine posts designed for extreme precision to wider posts for faster acquisition in dynamic situations. Rear sights also vary, with different notch widths and shapes. The goal is to find a combination that provides the best balance for your intended use. For precision marksmanship, a finer front sight post and a rear sight notch that provides a good, but not excessive, amount of light are often preferred. This allows for more precise placement of the front sight on a smaller aiming point. Conversely, for defensive shooting or action shooting, a wider front sight post and a notch that allows for more light might facilitate faster sight acquisition, as you're not trying to center a tiny post in a narrow gap. However, the principle of equal light remains constant, regardless of the specific sight dimensions.

The role of the eye in achieving proper sight alignment and sight picture cannot be overstated. The dominant eye plays a crucial role, and it is essential to understand which eye is your dominant one. For most people, it's the same as their dominant hand, but not always. A simple test to determine your dominant eye involves extending your arms forward, forming a triangle with your hands, and looking through that triangle at a distant object. Then, close one eye at a time. The eye that keeps the object aligned within your triangular frame is your dominant eye. Knowing your dominant eye is important because it's the eye that should be primarily focused on the sights. The non-dominant eye should be kept open or gently closed, and ideally, it should be trained to ignore the sights and focus on the target, allowing the dominant eye to provide the clear, sharp image of the sights.

Another critical aspect is where your eye focuses. When looking at your sights, the front sight should be sharp and in focus, while the rear sight should be slightly less sharp, and the target should be the least sharp of the three. This might seem counterintuitive, as we often think of focusing on the target. However, the physics of the eye dictate that it can only bring one plane into sharp focus at a time. The front sight is the most critical element to be in sharp focus because it is the most proximal reference point for the bore axis. If the front sight is blurry, your alignment will be compromised. If the target is in sharp focus, the front sight will necessarily be blurry, making precise alignment impossible. Therefore, the visual effort must be directed at the front sight, ensuring it is clear, crisp, and correctly positioned within the rear sight. The blurriness of the target is acceptable and, in fact, necessary for achieving accurate sight alignment and picture.

The concept of "target focus" is often a point of confusion for new shooters. When we're discussing sight picture, we are indeed placing the aligned sights *on* the target. However, the *act of aiming* requires focus on the sights, particularly the front sight. Once the correct sight picture is established – meaning the aligned sights are precisely where you want them to be on the target – the trigger press must be executed without disturbing that image. If you try to focus sharply on the target, your front sight will blur, and your alignment will suffer. The goal is to achieve a precise alignment of sights, place that alignment on the target, and then execute the trigger press while maintaining sharp focus on the front sight. The target will be visible, but in a slightly softer focus.

Let's explore practical ways to achieve and maintain this crucial alignment and picture. Dry-fire practice is an invaluable tool. With an unloaded firearm, you can practice acquiring your sight picture repeatedly. The goal is to develop the muscle memory and visual cues that allow you to bring the firearm up and automatically achieve the correct sight alignment and placement on a designated point (even if it's just a blank wall or a small aiming mark). Start by pointing the firearm in a safe direction and bringing it up to eye level. Focus on the front sight. Adjust your grip and the firearm's position until the front sight is perfectly centered within the rear sight, with equal light on both sides. Then, slowly move the firearm, keeping the front sight perfectly aligned and centered, and place it on your intended aiming point. Repeat this process hundreds, even thousands, of times. The goal is to make this process so automatic that you can do it quickly and consistently, even under stress.

When transitioning to live fire, the principles remain the same, but the added elements of recoil, noise, and the pressure of the shot itself can disrupt your carefully honed sight picture. This is where the follow-through we discussed previously becomes inextricably linked. Maintaining your sight picture *through* the shot, and even after the shot breaks, is essential.

Do not break your focus on the front sight immediately after the trigger press. Continue to hold your sight alignment and focus on the front sight as the firearm recoils. Observe where the sights naturally come to rest. This feedback loop is crucial for learning and improvement. If you release your focus too early, you won't know if your sight alignment was correct at the moment of firing, and you won't be able to diagnose potential issues effectively.

The type of sights on your firearm can also influence how you achieve sight alignment and sight picture. For instance, iron sights, as we've discussed, require meticulous alignment of post and notch. However, modern optics, such as red dot sights, introduce a different paradigm. With a red dot sight, there is no rear sight to align with. The "sight" is a single point of light (the red dot) projected onto a lens. The principle of sight picture still applies – the red dot must be placed on the target. However, the alignment aspect is largely absent, as there's no secondary reference point. The challenge then becomes ensuring the red dot is visible and centered within the optic's field of view when you bring the firearm up. This often involves "presenting" the firearm to your eye, rather than bringing your eye to the firearm, to ensure the dot appears naturally and consistently.

The focus here shifts to the consistent presentation of the firearm and the clear visualization of the red dot.

Furthermore, shooting in different lighting conditions presents challenges. In low light, the front sight might become less distinct, and the rear sight notch can be harder to discern. This can make achieving that critical "equal light" difficult. Some sights are designed with tritium inserts or fiber optic elements to aid in low-light visibility. Tritium sights offer a glowing dot or line that is visible in complete darkness, while fiber optic sights gather ambient light to create a brighter sight picture. When using these types of sights, you still strive for the same alignment principles, but the enhanced visibility of the sight elements can make the process more manageable. Even with illuminated sights, however, the fundamental principle of placing the front sight correctly within the rear sight remains.

For those employing a more advanced aiming system like a magnified scope on a rifle, the principles of sight alignment and sight picture take on a different form, often referred to as "scope mounting" and "eye relief." However, the core concept of establishing a clear, consistent line of sight to the target remains. The reticle within the scope must be properly aligned with the shooter's line of vision and placed precisely on the desired point of impact.

The "equal light" concept is replaced by ensuring the reticle is centered within the field of view, and the shooter achieves consistent eye relief (the distance between the eyepiece and the shooter's eye) to avoid a "scope shadow" or a distorted image.

Consider the practical application during a defensive scenario. Time is of the essence. You may not have the luxury of meticulously aligning your sights for several seconds. This is where the value of consistent, high-volume dry-fire and live-fire practice comes into play. Your ability to achieve correct sight alignment and picture under duress is a direct result of the neuromuscular pathways you've built through repetition. The goal is to reach a point where acquiring a good sight picture is an almost subconscious process, allowing your conscious mind to focus on the broader tactical picture – threat assessment, environmental awareness, and the decision to shoot.

A common pitfall for shooters is the tendency to "chase" the front sight, meaning they move their head or body to try and get the front sight perfectly centered in the rear sight, often at the expense of maintaining a stable shooting platform. The correct approach is to adjust the firearm in your hands and your body's position to bring the sights into alignment, rather than moving your head excessively. Think of it as bringing the firearm to your eye in a consistent manner each time you draw and aim.

The visual processing of sight alignment and sight picture is deeply intertwined with cognitive load. When you are under stress, your ability to process visual information can be impaired. Practicing under simulated stress, or simply practicing consistently until the process becomes automatic, helps to reduce this cognitive load. The more you can make the mechanics of aiming a background process, the more mental capacity you will have for critical decision-making.

Ultimately, achieving precision aim through sight alignment and sight picture is not a singular event but a continuous process of refinement. It requires discipline, patience, and a willingness to meticulously examine your own performance. Every shot fired is an opportunity to reinforce good habits or to identify areas for improvement. By understanding the physics involved, the role of your own visual system, and by diligently applying the principles of correct alignment and picture, you build the foundation for consistent accuracy. This foundation is not built overnight, but through dedicated practice and a keen awareness of the subtle yet critical relationship between your sights and your target. It is the bedrock upon which all advanced marksmanship skills are built.

Breathing Control for Steady Aim

The stillness required for a precise shot is not merely a static state; it is an actively managed condition, and at its core lies the mastery of your own physiology, specifically your breath. While we've meticulously examined the visual alignment of sights and their placement upon the target, the physical act of holding that perfect sight picture steady is profoundly influenced by our respiratory cycle. Without controlling our breath, even the most perfectly aligned sights will be subject to the subtle, yet often dramatic, movements of our diaphragm and chest. This is where the science and art of breathing control become paramount for the marksman seeking consistent accuracy.

Our bodies are in a constant state of natural respiration, a rhythmic process driven by the need to exchange oxygen and carbon dioxide. This rhythm, however, is not conducive to the static precision demanded by marksmanship. Every inhale and exhale causes a slight, albeit natural, expansion and contraction of the torso. When this movement is not accounted for, it directly translates to unwanted movement of the firearm, disrupting that hard-won sight picture just as the trigger is pressed. The key to overcoming this is to identify and exploit the brief moments of stillness that occur within this natural breathing cycle.

This period of stillness is often referred to as the "natural respiratory pause." It occurs momentarily after you exhale and before you begin to inhale again. Imagine taking a deep breath, then exhaling completely. For a fleeting second or two, your chest and abdomen will naturally remain relatively still before the urge to inhale signals the next cycle. This is your window of opportunity. It's a tiny pocket of tranquility within the ceaseless ebb and flow of respiration, and it is precisely during this pause that the steady aim is best achieved. Think of it as a brief, natural suspension of movement that your body provides, which you can then leverage for optimal shooting stability.

The practice of utilizing the natural respiratory pause involves a conscious, deliberate management of your breathing. It is not about holding your breath indefinitely, which can lead to increased muscle tension and even dizziness, but rather about synchronizing your shot with the body's natural pause. The process typically begins with taking a normal breath, not a forced, deep gasp, but a comfortable, measured breath. Then, you exhale smoothly and completely. As you reach the end of your exhalation, just before you feel the immediate need to inhale again, you find that moment of stillness. This is when you should execute your trigger press.

The firearm should be already aligned on the target, with your sights in perfect picture, and your finger should be initiating the smooth, consistent trigger pull during this pause.

Integrating this breathing technique with the trigger press is a skill that requires significant practice and mental discipline. The goal is to make the timing almost subconscious. Initially, you will need to actively think about each step: breathe in, exhale, pause, press the trigger. However, with repetition, this sequence will become more fluid. A common mistake is to try and hold the pause for too long, forcing your body to strain and thus introducing tension. The natural pause is fleeting; you must be prepared to act within that brief timeframe. This means having your sights aligned and your finger in position on the trigger *before* you reach the pause. The trigger press itself should then be initiated and completed *during* that natural stillness.

Let's break down the mechanics of this integration. As you begin your exhale, you should already be bringing the firearm to your shoulder and acquiring your sight picture. This allows you to use the time while exhaling to refine your aim. Once your sights are aligned and positioned correctly on the target, and you have exhaled to the point of that natural pause, you then apply smooth, increasing pressure to the trigger.

The trigger break should ideally occur within that moment of stillness. Immediately after the trigger breaks, you can resume your normal breathing cycle, and if necessary, reacquire your sight picture for a follow-up shot, again utilizing the natural respiratory pause.

The emphasis here is on a smooth, controlled exhale. Holding your breath forcefully can lead to a buildup of carbon dioxide in your bloodstream, which can cause shakiness and a feeling of panic or urgency. This is counterproductive to the calm, steady state required for marksmanship. Instead, aim for a relaxed, controlled exhalation. Visualize expelling tension from your body as you exhale. This mental aspect, coupled with the physical act of breathing, can significantly contribute to overall stability.

Dry-fire practice is an exceptionally effective method for developing this breathing control. Without the distractions of recoil and noise, you can focus purely on the rhythm of your breath and the timing of your trigger press. Set up a safe dry-fire environment. Practice drawing your firearm and acquiring your sight picture. Then, focus on your breathing. Exhale, pause, and execute a dry trigger press. Pay close attention to any body movement or tension that arises during this process. Do you feel your shoulders tense up? Does your head move?

Are you involuntarily jerking the trigger? By isolating these variables during dry-fire, you can systematically address them. Repeat this hundreds of times. The objective is to build the neuromuscular pathways that allow you to naturally time your trigger press with your natural respiratory pause. When transitioning to live fire, the challenge increases due to the sensory input of the gunshot and recoil. However, the principles remain the same. The recoil itself can sometimes help reset your breathing pattern. After the shot, allow your body to naturally take its next breath. For follow-up shots, you'll again aim to utilize that natural respiratory pause. The key is not to rush the process. Even in a dynamic situation, a fraction of a second spent managing your breath can yield a significantly more accurate shot.

It is also important to understand that different shooting disciplines and scenarios may necessitate slight variations in breathing technique. For extremely long-range precision shooting, where time is less of a constraint and absolute stillness is paramount, some shooters might advocate for a slightly longer breath hold *after* the natural pause, carefully controlled to minimize physiological strain. However, for the vast majority of practical shooting applications, including self-defense and general marksmanship, adhering to the natural respiratory pause is the most effective and sustainable method. It avoids the physiological consequences of forced breath-holding and works in harmony with your body's natural rhythms.

The concept of a "stable platform" in marksmanship extends beyond the grip and stance to include internal stability, and breath control is a critical component of that internal stability. When your breathing is erratic or uncontrolled, it creates internal oscillations that are transmitted through your body to the firearm. By mastering the natural respiratory pause, you are essentially minimizing these internal oscillations at the most opportune moment. This creates a more consistent and predictable platform from which to launch the projectile.

Consider the mental aspect. The act of consciously controlling your breath can have a calming effect. In stressful situations, our breathing often becomes shallow and rapid, a hallmark of the "fight or flight" response. By deliberately slowing and deepening your breath, and then finding that moment of stillness, you are actively counteracting this stress response. This can lead to clearer thinking, reduced anxiety, and a greater capacity to focus on the task at hand. Thus, breathing control is not just a physical technique; it's a mental management tool as well.

Some individuals may find it beneficial to practice specific breathing exercises outside of shooting drills to enhance their overall breath control. Techniques such as diaphragmatic breathing, where you focus on expanding your abdomen rather than just your chest, can improve lung capacity and promote a more relaxed breathing pattern. Mindfulness and meditation practices can also cultivate a greater awareness of your body's natural rhythms, including your breath, making it easier to identify and utilize the natural respiratory pause when shooting.

The visual focus we discussed in previous sections remains critical. While you are managing your breath and preparing to press the trigger, your primary visual attention should still be on the front sight, ensuring it remains perfectly aligned and focused. The breath control and trigger press are happening concurrently with this visual focus. It's a multi-faceted skill set that needs to be integrated seamlessly. You're not just breathing; you're breathing *while* aiming, *while* holding steady, and *while* executing a smooth trigger press.

For newer shooters, the concept of breathing control might seem like an overly complex addition to an already demanding skill. However, it is one of the most impactful techniques for improving shot-to-shot consistency.

Ignoring it is akin to building a house on an unstable foundation. You can erect walls and a roof, but the structure will always be vulnerable to tremors. Breathing control provides that solid foundation for your marksmanship. It is a fundamental building block that, when integrated with proper sight alignment, sight picture, and trigger control, elevates your performance from inconsistent to consistently accurate. It transforms the act of shooting from a reactive event to a controlled and deliberate execution. The steady aim is not achieved by sheer force of will, but by intelligently working with, and momentarily pausing, the very rhythm of life itself.

Understanding and Utilizing Eye Dominance

The consistent placement of your firearm's sights on the target is the bedrock of accurate shooting. We've delved into the intricacies of sight alignment and sight picture, understanding how the front sight must be perfectly centered within the rear sight aperture, and how both must then be crisply focused on the point of aim. Yet, the process of achieving this perfect alignment and holding it steady is inherently tied to our own physiology, specifically the way our eyes work together. This is where the concept of eye dominance enters the arena of marksmanship, playing a critical, though often overlooked, role in developing a repeatable and precise aiming process.

For centuries, marksmanship has been refined through understanding and mastering the tool – the firearm – and the environment. However, a significant leap in proficiency comes from understanding and mastering the most vital tool of all: the shooter themselves. And within that self-mastery, the eyes are paramount.

Eye dominance, in essence, is the preference of one eye over the other for visual input when both eyes are open. Think of it as your brain's default setting for processing visual information for tasks requiring fine motor skills and precise targeting. Just as most people have a dominant hand for writing or throwing, most individuals also have a dominant eye. This dominant eye is the one that provides the clearest, most consistent visual input, and it's the eye your brain will naturally favor when aiming. This preference isn't a conscious choice; it's an ingrained neurological pathway. When you aim a firearm, your brain instinctively wants to use the input from your dominant eye to achieve that precise sight alignment and focus on the target. Understanding and leveraging this natural inclination is key to developing a consistent shooting technique. For the vast majority of people, their dominant eye will be on the same side as their dominant hand – a right-handed shooter typically has a dominant right eye, and a left-handed shooter, a dominant left eye. However, this is not universally true. A significant portion of the population exhibits a phenomenon known as cross-dominance, where their dominant eye is opposite to their dominant hand. This can present unique challenges and require specific adaptations in shooting technique, but it is by no means a barrier to becoming an accurate shooter. The critical importance of eye dominance in marksmanship stems directly from how we aim. When you bring a firearm to your shoulder and look through the sights, your dominant eye is the one that will naturally achieve the clearest and most stable sight picture. If you attempt to aim with your non-dominant eye, your brain will often struggle to reconcile the visual input from both eyes, leading to a less precise alignment, a blurry sight picture, or even a sensation of double vision or misalignment that can cause you to subconsciously shift your head position to try and "correct" it. This subconscious adjustment is detrimental to consistency. The goal of marksmanship is repeatability, and that repeatability is built upon a stable and consistent platform, which includes a consistent cheek weld and consistent eye placement relative to the sights. Your eye dominance directly influences how you should position yourself to achieve that consistent platform. Without acknowledging eye dominance, a shooter might unknowingly be fighting their own physiology, leading to frustration and reduced accuracy.

Fortunately, determining your eye dominance is a straightforward process that can be performed with minimal equipment and without any specialized knowledge. These simple tests are designed to leverage the natural tendency of your brain to favor one eye when focusing on a distant point. It's crucial to perform these tests with both eyes open initially, as this simulates the actual aiming process more closely. The goal is to isolate which eye is providing the primary visual reference.

One of the most common and effective tests involves creating a "peephole" or window with your hands. Stand at a distance of about 10-15 feet from a fixed object across the room a picture on the wall, a light switch, or even a doorknob will suffice. Extend your arms forward and bring your hands together to form a triangular or circular opening with your thumbs and forefingers, creating a window through which to view the target. Now, with both eyes open, aim this window at the distant object. Focus on the object through the opening. Once you have a clear, singular image of the object in your "window," close your right eye. If the object remains centered in your window, your left eye is likely your dominant eye. Now, keeping your left eye closed, open your right eye. If the object shifts out of the window or you lose your precise aim, it further confirms that your left eye is your dominant eye.

Conversely, if closing your left eye causes the object to shift, and keeping it closed while opening your right eye maintains the aim, then your right eye is dominant. This test works because when your dominant eye is open, your brain uses its input to keep the object aligned within the frame you've created with your hands. When you close your dominant eye, your non-dominant eye attempts to take over, but your brain's ingrained preference causes a slight shift in perception or physical alignment, and the target is no longer perfectly framed.

Another equally effective method is the "pointing test." Again, find a distant object. Extend your arm straight out in front of you, with your index finger pointing towards the object. Keep your arm straight and your finger pointing. Now, with both eyes open, focus on the object and ensure your finger is precisely on it. Once you have this established, without moving your arm or finger, close your right eye. If your finger remains on the target, your left eye is dominant. Then, keeping your left eye closed, open your right eye. If your finger appears to shift away from the target, it further validates your left eye as dominant. If closing your left eye causes your finger to deviate from the target, and opening your right eye (while keeping the left closed) keeps your finger aligned, then your right eye is dominant.

This test relies on the same principle: your dominant eye provides the primary visual reference, and when it's closed, your brain has to rely on the less preferred eye, leading to a perceived or actual shift in your aim.

A third, and perhaps even simpler, test can be done by simply looking at a distant object and making a circle with your thumb and index finger. Extend your arm and place the circle around the object. Then, close one eye at a time. The eye that allows you to keep the object perfectly framed within the circle is your dominant eye. This is a variation of the first test but can be done more quickly. Remember to perform these tests carefully and without forcing your eyes. The results should feel natural, not strained. If you consistently get the same result across multiple tests, you can be confident in identifying your dominant eye. It's also worth noting that eye dominance can, in rare cases, change over time or be influenced by factors such as injury or certain medical conditions, but for the vast majority of individuals, it remains consistent.

Once you have confidently identified your dominant eye, the next step is to understand how this impacts your shooting technique and what adjustments might be necessary. For shooters who are right-handed and right-eye dominant, or left-handed and left-eye dominant, the alignment is straightforward.

You will simply bring the firearm up to your dominant eye, placing your cheek firmly against the stock or frame in a consistent manner. This natural alignment ensures that your dominant eye is directly behind the sights, providing the clearest and most stable sight picture. The cheek weld becomes intuitive, as your dominant eye naturally finds its place behind the rear sight.

The complexity and the need for specific techniques arise when a shooter is cross-dominant. For example, a right-handed shooter who is left-eye dominant. In this scenario, if they try to shoot a right-handed rifle, their dominant left eye will naturally want to align with the sights, which are positioned on the right side of the firearm. This forces the shooter to either cant their head significantly to the right, breaking a proper cheek weld and introducing instability, or closing their left eye, which means they are aiming with their non-dominant right eye. Aiming with the non-dominant eye is significantly more challenging and can lead to inconsistent accuracy, fuzzy sight pictures, and increased shooter fatigue.

For a cross-dominant shooter, there are several viable paths forward, each with its own advantages and considerations. The first, and often the most direct, approach is to learn to shoot with your non-dominant eye.

This requires dedicated practice and a conscious effort to overcome the natural inclination of your dominant eye. When aiming, you would close your dominant eye and rely solely on your non-dominant eye. This means ensuring your cheek weld is set up so your non-dominant eye is directly behind the sights. The initial stages of this might feel awkward, and you might find yourself subconsciously wanting to open your dominant eye. Consistency is achieved through repetition and a deliberate focus on using only the non-dominant eye for sighting. This method is often preferred by those who are committed to a particular firearm platform (e.g., a right-handed pistol shooter who wants to remain right-handed).

The second approach for a cross-dominant shooter, particularly with long guns like rifles and shotguns, is to simply switch the dominant side for which the firearm is configured. A right-handed, left-eye dominant shooter could learn to shoot a left-handed rifle. This allows their dominant left eye to naturally align with the sights. This requires a different manual of arms for manipulating the firearm (e.g., operating the bolt with their left hand), but it can lead to a more natural and comfortable aiming process. For pistols, this would mean learning to shoot with their left hand, which again allows their dominant left eye to align with the sights.

This is a perfectly valid and effective solution for many, though it does require adapting manual dexterity to the non-dominant side.

A third strategy, often employed by both rifle and pistol shooters, involves adapting the shooting position or using specific techniques to accommodate eye dominance. For long guns, this can involve intentionally canting the firearm slightly or adjusting the cheek weld to position the head at an angle that allows the dominant eye to see the sights properly. This is a delicate balance, as you must maintain a solid and repeatable cheek weld while still achieving correct eye placement. It's about finding that sweet spot where your dominant eye is positioned correctly behind the sights without compromising the stability of your platform. For handguns, this can sometimes involve a slightly more pronounced "face-to-the-gun" method, where the shooter brings their face more fully onto the grip, allowing the dominant eye to naturally fall into alignment.

Another technique, particularly relevant for pistol shooters, is the use of an occluding device or method. This involves physically blocking the vision of the non-dominant eye while aiming. A simple and effective method is to use a small piece of opaque tape placed over the lens of shooting glasses on the side of the non-dominant eye.

When you bring the pistol up and look through the sights, the tape will block the input from your non-dominant eye, forcing your brain to rely on the input from your dominant eye. This is not about closing the eye, but about preventing visual distraction from that side. This allows a right-handed shooter who is left-eye dominant to shoot a right-handed pistol while ensuring their dominant left eye is the one doing the aiming. The tape can be easily removed when not shooting. Alternatively, some shooters use a small, adhesive occluder that can be applied directly to the lens of their glasses. This method is often favored because it allows the shooter to maintain an open, relaxed eye, which can be less fatiguing than actively closing an eye for extended periods. It's important to ensure that the occluding device is positioned correctly so it effectively blocks the visual field of the non-dominant eye without obstructing your peripheral vision on the dominant side.

It is absolutely critical to reiterate that for any shooter, regardless of dominance, the *dominant eye* must be the one used for aiming. The brain relies on that primary visual input for precision. The challenge of eye dominance arises when the dominant eye is not naturally aligned with the shooting side of the firearm. The goal is always to get your dominant eye directly behind the sights, forming that clear sight picture.

Whether you achieve this by learning to shoot with your non-dominant hand, by adjusting your head position, or by using an occluding device, the fundamental principle remains the same: your dominant eye is your aiming eye.

The concept of the "cheek weld" becomes particularly important when discussing eye dominance. A proper cheek weld is the firm, consistent contact of your cheek against the comb of the rifle stock or the backstrap of a handgun. This contact point is crucial for establishing a stable shooting platform and ensuring your eye is always at the same distance and angle relative to the sights. For a shooter with natural eye-hand dominance alignment, achieving a proper cheek weld naturally places their dominant eye behind the sights. However, for a cross-dominant shooter who chooses to shoot with their dominant hand, they must consciously work to achieve a cheek weld that allows their *dominant eye* to align with the sights. This might mean a slightly different angle of the head or stock than what feels intuitively "square" if one were simply looking at the firearm from the front. It's about finding that repeatable position that puts your dominant eye in the correct position.

A common mistake for new shooters, especially those who are cross-dominant, is to simply close their dominant eye and try to aim with their non-dominant eye without any specific training.

While it might seem like the logical solution, it often leads to poor accuracy because the non-dominant eye is not as adept at fine visual discrimination for aiming. The brain may also struggle to suppress the input from the dominant eye, leading to a fluctuating or uncertain sight picture. Therefore, if you are determined to shoot with your non-dominant eye, it requires dedicated practice. Focus on keeping your dominant eye closed and actively using your non-dominant eye to acquire and maintain the sight picture. Start with slow, deliberate shots and gradually increase the pace as your proficiency improves.

Furthermore, understanding eye dominance is not just about identifying it; it's about integrating that knowledge into your practice routine. When you are dry-firing, pay close attention to how your eye alignment changes as you bring the firearm up. If you notice your head tilting or your eye moving off-center, consider whether this is related to your eye dominance and how you are compensating. During live-fire practice, consciously assess your sight picture. Is it consistently clear? Are you having to adjust your head position more than you think you should? These are all clues that might point to an issue with eye dominance or how you are addressing it.

The beauty of understanding and addressing eye dominance is that it removes a significant variable from the equation of accuracy. Once you know your dominant eye and have established a consistent method for aligning it with your sights, you can then focus on refining other aspects of your marksmanship, such as breath control and trigger management, with greater confidence. It is about creating a system that works with your body, not against it. Don't be discouraged if you discover you are cross-dominant; many highly skilled shooters are. It simply means you may need to put a bit more thought and practice into finding the technique that best suits your unique physiology. The goal is always to achieve that perfect, repeatable sight picture, and understanding your eye dominance is a fundamental step in making that a reality. It's a crucial piece of the puzzle that ensures your visual system is working in harmony with your firearm and your target, leading to more consistent and confident shots.

Proficiency of One-Handed Shooting

The mastery of firearm manipulation extends beyond the ideal conditions of a controlled range environment. While two-handed shooting provides a stable platform and superior control, the reality of critical incidents often dictates that a firearm must be employed with a single hand. This might occur due to injury to the strong hand, the need to maintain control of a child or another person, the necessity of performing other tasks simultaneously, or simply the dynamic nature of a confrontation where a two-handed grip is not feasible. Proficiency in one-handed shooting is not merely an advanced technique; it is a fundamental component of comprehensive tactical preparedness, offering a critical advantage when circumstances demand it.

The fundamental challenges in one-handed shooting are rooted in physics and human physiology. With only one hand on the firearm, the shooter loses significant leverage and control over grip pressure and muzzle rise. The recoil impulse, which is managed and absorbed more effectively by the coordinated effort of two hands, becomes a much more significant disruptive force. This increased muzzle rise can lead to a loss of sight alignment between shots, significantly impacting follow-up accuracy. Furthermore, the grip itself becomes more tenuous. The non-dominant hand, typically used to reinforce the grip and control the firearm's movement, is absent, placing a greater burden on the fingers and thumb of the shooting hand to maintain a secure hold. The mental component is also substantial; shooting one-handed often feels less stable and requires a heightened degree of concentration and proprioceptive awareness to manage the firearm effectively.

To address these challenges, the approach to grip becomes paramount. For a right-handed shooter, this means employing the right hand to hold and operate the pistol. The grip should be firm and high on the backstrap of the pistol, allowing the web of your hand to sit as high as possible. This positioning helps to control the upward rotation of the muzzle under recoil. The thumb of the shooting hand should rest along the side of the pistol, often extending parallel to the bore line or slightly angled. Avoid wrapping the thumb aggressively over the top of the slide or the controls, as this can impede slide function or accidentally engage the magazine release. The fingers should be wrapped firmly around the grip, applying consistent pressure. The goal is to create a "vise like" grip that minimizes the ability of the pistol to rotate upwards in your hand. This requires conscious effort to maintain tension in the shooting hand and forearm throughout the firing sequence. For left-handed shooters, the same principles apply in reverse, using the left hand to grip and control the firearm. The key is to maximize the surface area of contact and apply consistent, strong pressure.

Recoil management is where one-handed shooting truly tests a shooter's skill. Unlike two-handed shooting where the non-dominant hand acts as a shock absorber and counter-lever, in one-handed shooting, the entire burden falls on the shooting hand and wrist. The technique here involves a more proactive approach to absorbing recoil. As the shot is fired, the shooter must actively resist the muzzle's tendency to rise. This is not a passive process; it requires engaging the muscles in the wrist and forearm to create a firm, stable platform that can absorb and manage the energy. A strong wrist, kept straight and locked, is essential. Imagine your wrist as a rigid extension of your arm, rather than a flexible joint that bends under pressure. This straight wrist allows the recoil energy to be transferred more directly into your arm and shoulder, rather than causing the muzzle to flip upwards. Some shooters also find it beneficial to slightly "lean into" the shot, using their body weight to help stabilize the firearm, but this must be done without sacrificing balance or creating an unnatural shooting posture.

Maintaining sight alignment during one-handed shooting is significantly more difficult due to the increased muzzle rise. The front sight will naturally want to climb away from the rear sight after each shot. The shooter's task is to bring the front sight back down to the rear sight as quickly and efficiently as possible, ideally before the trigger is reset. This requires rapid target re-acquisition and a strong focus on the front sight. The goal is to have the front sight firmly re-seated within the rear sight aperture, aligned with the point of aim, for each subsequent shot. This is where practice and repetition are absolutely critical. Drills that focus on drawing the firearm, firing a single shot, and then re-acquiring the sight picture for a follow-up shot are invaluable. The emphasis should be on the speed and consistency of returning the sights to alignment, not necessarily on extreme speed of fire initially. Accuracy is the priority, and speed will naturally follow with proficiency.

The role of the non-dominant hand in a one-handed shooting scenario is not entirely absent, even though it is not on the firearm. If the non-dominant hand is free, it can be used for support and stability. In some instances, the non-dominant hand can be used to "press" into the shooter's body, on their chest or hip, to create a more stable shooting platform. This is akin to using a braced position, where the non-dominant hand provides an anchor point. In other situations, if the non-dominant hand is occupied, for example, holding a child or an object, the shooter must adapt by focusing solely on the grip and recoil management with the shooting hand. The goal is to be able to perform effectively regardless of the status of the non-dominant hand.

Developing proficiency in one-handed shooting requires a dedicated and structured training approach. One of the foundational drills is the "one-shot draw and fire."

This drill emphasizes the mechanics of drawing the firearm cleanly, establishing a firm grip, and firing a single accurate shot. The focus here is on the process: the draw, the grip, the sight alignment, the trigger press, and then the conscious management of recoil. After each shot, the shooter should consciously check their sight alignment and prepare for the next shot. This drill can be performed at various distances, starting close to the target and gradually increasing the range as comfort and accuracy improve.

Another crucial drill is the "emergency reload" practiced with a single hand. If the pistol runs dry, a reload must be executed without the assistance of the non-dominant hand. This means that the shooter must be able to drop the empty magazine, retrieve a fresh one from a magazine pouch, insert it into the magazine well, and rack the slide or release the slide if the slide is already locked back, all using only the shooting hand. This is a complex sequence of fine motor skills that becomes significantly more challenging under stress. Practicing this sequence slowly and deliberately, without ammunition, is the first step. Once the sequence is memorized and can be executed smoothly, it can be incorporated into live-fire drills. The ability to perform a one-handed reload is essential for maintaining offensive capability.

Follow-up shots are the core of effective one-handed shooting. Drills that focus on rapid, accurate follow-up shots are vital. The "Bill Drill," a classic drill that involves firing ten shots at a target from ten yards in ten seconds, can be adapted for one-handed shooting. While achieving ten shots in ten seconds with one hand might be an advanced goal, the principle of rapid, accurate fire is what's important. Focus on bringing the sights back into alignment quickly after each shot. Don't sacrifice accuracy for speed. Initially, aim for achieving a solid sight picture for each shot, even if it means firing more slowly. As your control improves, you can begin to increase the tempo. Another effective drill is the "transition drill," where the shooter fires a single shot from two hands, then transitions to one hand and fires additional shots. This helps the shooter understand the differences in control and accuracy between the two shooting positions.

When practicing one-handed shooting, it is also important to consider the type of firearm being used. Smaller, lighter pistols are inherently more difficult to control with one hand due to their lower mass and higher recoil relative to their size. Larger, heavier pistols, particularly those with longer barrels and a lower bore axis, tend to be easier to manage.

However, the principles of grip, recoil management, and sight acquisition remain the same regardless of the firearm. The goal is to adapt your technique to the tool you have. For those considering a firearm for self-defense where one-handed shooting might be a frequent necessity, selecting a pistol that balances concealability with shootability is crucial.

The mental aspect of one-handed shooting cannot be overstated. It requires a higher level of focus and a deliberate acceptance of the diminished control. Shooters must train themselves to remain calm and focused, despite the increased muzzle flip and potential for less precise follow-up shots. Visualization plays a significant role. Mentally rehearsing the sequence of a one-handed shot, from the draw to the follow-up, can build confidence and prepare the shooter for the physical demands. Understanding that perfect accuracy might not be achievable with every single shot in a rapid, one-handed sequence is also important. The goal is to place enough effective shots on target to neutralize the threat, not necessarily to achieve bullseyes with every round.

It is also important to consider the type of ammunition used. Heavier bullets with moderate velocities often provide a more manageable recoil impulse compared to very light, high-velocity rounds, which can feel "snappy."

However, this is a secondary consideration, and focusing on mastering the fundamental shooting techniques is far more important than experimenting with different ammunition types, especially in the initial stages of training.

Finally, the process of learning and refining one-handed shooting skills should be progressive. Begin with fundamental drills, focusing on grip, sight alignment, and controlled trigger press. As you become more comfortable, introduce drills that simulate more dynamic scenarios. Always prioritize safety and ensure that you are training in a controlled environment with qualified instruction. The ability to effectively employ a firearm with a single hand is a testament to a well-rounded shooter's preparedness, an essential skill that can make a critical difference when facing the unpredictable realities of a defensive encounter. It demands attention to detail, a willingness to embrace discomfort, and a commitment to rigorous practice, but the reward is enhanced survivability and confidence in a wider range of circumstances.

Introduction to Malfunction Drills and Reloading Techniques

The transition from ensuring a firearm is operational to maintaining its operational capacity under duress is where proficiency truly takes root. While the previous discussions have focused on acquiring a stable shooting platform and managing recoil, the finite nature of ammunition and the potential for mechanical failures demand a parallel set of skills: effective reloading and malfunction clearing. These are not merely supplementary techniques; they are integral components of firearms handling that, when honed, can mean the difference between success and failure in a critical situation. The ability to quickly and efficiently bring a firearm back into a firing state after expending its ammunition or encountering a stoppage is a hallmark of a prepared individual.

Let us first delve into the realm of reloading. In a defensive encounter, the moment a firearm runs dry is a moment of extreme vulnerability. There is no time to calmly disassemble the pistol or fumble for a fresh magazine. This is where the concept of the "speed reload" becomes paramount. A speed reload is executed when the firearm has been emptied, and the slide is locked to the rear or the cylinder is open. The objective is to replace the empty magazine or cylinder with a loaded one as rapidly as possible, minimizing the time spent in a non-firing state. The mechanics of a speed reload begin the instant the shooter perceives the "click" of an empty chamber or empty magazine.

The first step in a speed reload, assuming a semi-automatic pistol, is to ensure the slide is indeed locked to the rear.

If it is not, a deliberate action to lock it back is necessary, though in many modern firearms, an empty magazine will cause the slide to lock automatically. With the slide locked back, the shooter's primary hand, which is still gripping the pistol, must disengage the magazine catch. This is typically achieved by pressing the magazine release button with the thumb of the shooting hand. Simultaneously, or in very rapid succession, the shooting hand moves to eject the empty magazine. This is not a gentle pull; it is a firm, downward motion to dislodge the magazine, allowing gravity to assist its exit. It is crucial to ensure a clean release of the empty magazine. Dropping it carelessly can result in it falling onto the ground in a manner that might impede its retrieval later, or worse, it could snag on clothing or gear.

While the empty magazine is being released, the non-dominant hand, which has been actively assisting in the shooting process or has moved to a neutral position, now moves to retrieve a fresh magazine. This magazine should be prepositioned in its pouch for a rapid, consistent draw. The grip on the fresh magazine is critical: fingers should be wrapped around the body of the magazine, with the thumb and index finger positioned to facilitate a smooth insertion into the magazine well.

Some practitioners advocate for a "pinky forward" grip on the magazine, where the little finger of the non-dominant hand is extended, ready to guide the magazine directly into the pistol's mag well. This can aid in alignment and prevent the magazine from striking the front of the mag well and causing a malfunction.

The insertion of the fresh magazine is a deliberate action. The shooter must guide the magazine into the well, ensuring it seats fully. This means pushing it upwards until it is flush with the bottom of the pistol's grip or until the magazine catch engages. A positive "thunk" or click often indicates that the magazine is properly seated. However, simply seating the magazine is not enough. The slide must be released to chamber a round. This can be achieved in several ways, depending on the firearm and shooter preference. The most common methods are using the slide release lever on the pistol or performing a "slingshot" reload.

The slide release lever method involves using the thumb of the shooting hand (or the index finger of the non-dominant hand, depending on grip and firearm design) to depress the slide release, allowing the slide to slam forward under the tension of the recoil spring, chambering a round. The slingshot method, favored by many, involves grabbing the slide of the pistol with the thumb and fingers of the non-dominant hand, pulling it fully to the rear, and then rapidly releasing it. This motion, when performed correctly, is often more reliable, especially for shooters who may have difficulty operating the slide release lever under stress or with certain firearm models. It also reinforces the grip of the non-dominant hand on the firearm, making it easier to transition back into a firing grip.

The transition back to a firing grip after a speed reload is just as important as the reload itself. The non-dominant hand, having released the slide or inserted the magazine, must move decisively to reinforce the grip on the pistol, re-establishing the two-handed shooting posture. This transition must be fluid and minimize any pause between the completion of the reload and the resumption of a stable shooting platform.

Beyond the speed reload, the "tactical reload" is another essential technique. A tactical reload is performed when the shooter has an opportunity to replenish their ammunition supply without being under immediate threat. This might occur during a lull in activity, or when transitioning between cover. The objective here is not pure speed, but rather efficient and maintaining a ready firearm. In a tactical reload, the shooter typically still has rounds in the pistol. The empty magazine is not simply dropped; it is retained.

The process for a tactical reload begins with the shooter observing that their magazine is low or making a conscious decision to reload during a safe period. The shooter then draws a fresh magazine from their pouch. Instead of immediately ejecting the partially or fully loaded magazine from the pistol, the shooter brings the pistol up towards their chest or a position of relative safety, while simultaneously inserting the fresh magazine into the magazine well. This insertion often pushes the partially loaded magazine out of the pistol, which the shooter then retains in their non-dominant hand. The pistol is then manipulated to chamber a round if necessary (e.g., if it was emptied), or if it still has rounds, the shooter can continue engaging targets. The partially expended magazine is then stowed, either back in its pouch or in a designated "dump pouch." The advantage of the tactical reload is that you maintain a loaded firearm throughout the process, and you retain the partially expended magazine, which can be used later if a speed reload becomes necessary. This is a more conservative approach that prioritizes ammunition management.

Transitioning between magazines or cylinders, particularly in revolvers, requires a different set of motions, but the underlying principles of efficiency and muscle memory remain.

For a revolver, this involves operating the cylinder release, which causes the cylinder to swing out from the frame. Then, spent casings are ejected, typically by a simple push on the ejector rod. A speedloader or moon clips can then be used to rapidly insert fresh rounds into the cylinder, which is then closed back into the frame. The process for revolvers, while seemingly different, also benefits immensely from dedicated practice to ensure smooth, repeatable actions.

The effectiveness of any reload or malfunction drill is significantly amplified by a fundamental understanding of situational awareness. Reloading or clearing a malfunction is not performed in a vacuum. The shooter must constantly scan their surroundings, be aware of their environment, and understand the threat landscape. This means that the reload or clearing process should ideally be performed while moving to cover, or while observing potential threats. A shooter who is entirely focused on the mechanics of their firearm, to the exclusion of their surroundings, is a vulnerable shooter. Therefore, drills should incorporate elements of scanning and observation. For instance, a shooter might be instructed to reload only after identifying a specific threat or after moving to a new piece of cover.

The concept of "malfunction drills" is equally critical. A firearm, being a mechanical device, can and will eventually fail. Understanding how to diagnose and clear common malfunctions quickly and efficiently is a non-negotiable skill for any firearm owner. The most common malfunction in semi-automatic pistols is often referred to as a "failure to feed" or "stovepipe." This occurs when a new round fails to chamber properly, often getting stuck between the slide and the breech face, with the rim of the cartridge case caught in the extractor.

The immediate response to a "stovepipe" malfunction is a two-step process often called "tap, rack, bang." First, the shooter must "tap" the bottom of the magazine to ensure it is fully seated. This is because a loose or improperly seated magazine is a common cause of feeding issues. Next, the shooter must "rack" the slide. This involves pulling the slide firmly to the rear, which will typically extract the offending round, and then releasing the slide to chamber a fresh round. Finally, the shooter attempts to "bang," which is to fire the pistol. If the malfunction is cleared, the firearm will function normally. This sequence must be practiced until it becomes an almost involuntary reaction. The emphasis here is on a firm, decisive action rather than a tentative one. A weak rack of the slide will often not clear the obstruction.

Another common malfunction is a "failure to extract," where a spent casing remains in the chamber and the slide attempts to chamber a new round, leading to a jam. Clearing this often requires a bit more manipulation. The slide is usually locked to the rear. The shooter might need to use a tool, or in some cases, the edge of a magazine or a finger, to physically dislodge the stuck casing from the chamber. Following this, the slide is released to chamber a new round, and the shooter attempts to fire.

Stoppages can also occur due to a variety of reasons, including poor quality ammunition, debris in the action, or even improper manipulation. The core principle in clearing any malfunction is to be systematic and deliberate. Rushing the process often exacerbates the problem. However, "deliberate" in this context does not mean slow; it means executing the correct steps with focus.

Practicing these drills, both dry-fire and live-fire, is essential. Dry-fire practice is invaluable for developing the muscle memory for magazine changes and slide manipulation without expending ammunition. It allows for repetition of the exact motions required without the cost or logistical challenges of live ammunition.

However, live-fire practice is crucial to experience the feel of the firearm cycling, the recoil, and the transition back to a firing grip under actual shooting conditions.

When practicing malfunction drills, it is highly beneficial to deliberately induce malfunctions. This can be done by using ammunition known to cause issues (though this should be done with caution and awareness), or by intentionally short-stroking the slide during live-fire. Experienced instructors can also set up drills where malfunctions are introduced at unexpected moments, forcing the shooter to react under pressure. The key is to simulate the stress of a real-world encounter as closely as possible.

The goal of mastering these reloading and malfunction clearing techniques is not simply to perform them, but to perform them *without conscious thought*. During a high-stress event, cognitive load is significantly increased. If a shooter has to stop and think, "Okay, now I need to press the magazine release, then grab the magazine, then insert the new one, then release the slide," they are expending valuable mental energy that could be better used assessing the threat. Through thousands of repetitions, these actions become ingrained. They become part of the shooter's reflexes, allowing them to maintain their focus on the critical task of defending themselves or others.

Furthermore, these drills should be integrated with other shooting fundamentals. A reload executed flawlessly, but with a poor grip or an inability to reacquire the sight picture, is still an ineffective reload. The proficiency gained in these advanced techniques must be layered upon a solid foundation of basic marksmanship and firearm control. The ability to transition seamlessly from firing to reloading or malfunction clearing, and then back to firing, is what separates a competent shooter from a truly proficient one. It is this seamless integration that builds confidence and ensures operational readiness in the face of adversity.

Chapter 6:

The Lifelong Commitment to Firearm Competency

Continuous Training the Path to Mastery

Firearm competency, much like any other highly refined skill, is not a static achievement but a dynamic process. It is a journey, not a destination, requiring constant engagement and deliberate effort to maintain and elevate proficiency. The initial acquisition of knowledge and the mastering of fundamental techniques, while crucial, represent only the foundational steps. True mastery lies in the unwavering commitment to continuous training and practice. Without this diligent, ongoing engagement, skills inevitably degrade. The muscle memory that was painstakingly built can fade, the rapid decision-making processes can slow, and the confidence that stems from proven ability can erode. Therefore, for any firearm owner who values safety, effectiveness, and their own peace of mind, embracing continuous learning is not merely recommended; it is an imperative.

The cornerstone of this ongoing development is regular, consistent practice. The shooting range, often viewed as the primary arena for live-fire training, is an indispensable resource.

However, the effectiveness of these range of visits are directly proportional to the intentionality of the practice. Simply sending rounds downrange without a specific objective is akin to exercising without a plan; it may offer some benefit, but its impact is limited. Instead, each trip to the range should be structured around specific skill sets. This might involve dedicating time to reinforcing fundamental marksmanship, such as grip, stance, and trigger control, perhaps by setting up drills that focus on accuracy at varying distances. It could also involve practicing the essential skills discussed previously, like reloading under simulated pressure or clearing malfunctions. Even dedicating a portion of a range session to shooting from different positions or engaging targets while moving can significantly enhance a shooter's adaptability and preparedness for real-world scenarios. The key is variety and purpose, ensuring that practice sessions challenge existing skills and introduce new layers of complexity.

Beyond the familiar environment of the local range, seeking out advanced training opportunities is a powerful catalyst for growth. The world of firearms instruction is rich with specialized courses that delve into areas far beyond basic marksmanship. These advanced courses, often led by seasoned professionals with extensive operational experience, can cover a broad spectrum of critical topics. Shooters might explore defensive pistol techniques that emphasize close-quarters engagement, rapid threat assessment, and shooting while moving. Others might focus on low-light shooting, introducing the challenges and techniques required to effectively identify and engage threats when visibility is compromised. Scenario-based training, a particularly valuable component of advanced instruction, immerses participants in simulated critical incidents, forcing them to make split-second decisions under intense psychological pressure. These courses provide a controlled environment to test and refine skills, receive expert feedback, and gain exposure to methodologies and perspectives that may not be apparent through self-study or basic training alone. The investment in these specialized courses is an investment in preparedness, pushing the boundaries of one's competency and building a more robust skill set.

While live-fire practice is undeniably essential for developing the physical and mental responses associated with shooting, the value of consistent dry-fire practice cannot be overstated. Dry-fire, the practice of manipulating a firearm without live ammunition, offers a unique and highly efficient avenue for skill development. It is cost-effective, accessible in almost any safe environment, and allows for an incredible volume of repetitions that would be impractical or prohibitively expensive with live ammunition. The fundamental aspects of firearm handling – drawing from a holster, acquiring a sight picture, performing a smooth trigger press, and executing reloads and malfunction clearances – can all be honed through diligent dry-fire drills. The key is to create a safe practice environment, ensuring the firearm is unloaded and that no ammunition is present in the vicinity. This allows for the development of crucial muscle memory. For instance, practicing the draw stroke repeatedly, focusing on each step from the grip on the firearm to the presentation of the weapon, builds fluidity and speed. Similarly, practicing magazine changes, ensuring each step – from actuating the magazine release to seating the new magazine and potentially manipulating the slide – is performed smoothly and efficiently, can be done hundreds of times in a single dry-fire session. The development of a consistent trigger press, without disturbing the sight picture, is another area where dry-fire excels. By focusing on a slow, controlled press that breaks the shot cleanly, shooters can build the dexterity and control necessary for accurate shooting. Furthermore, dry-fire is an excellent tool for familiarizing oneself with the nuances of a specific firearm, understanding its trigger pull characteristics, the location and function of its controls, and how to operate it efficiently.

This consistent, deliberate practice builds the subconscious proficiency that allows a shooter to react effectively under stress, rather than having to consciously think through each step.

The concept of "progressive training" is also a vital element of continuous skill development. This involves gradually increasing the complexity and demands of training exercises. For example, a shooter might begin by practicing reloads while standing still at a stationary target. Once that is mastered, they might progress to practicing reloads while moving from one point to another, or while transitioning between different shooting positions. Similarly, malfunction clearing drills can start with simply racking the slide for a stovepipe while standing still, and then evolve to clearing malfunctions while under simulated time pressure or while engaging multiple targets. This progressive overload ensures that skills are not only maintained but are constantly being tested and improved against increasing challenges. It prevents complacency and ensures that the shooter is prepared for a wider range of eventualities.

Another critical aspect of continuous training is the commitment to understanding the operational mechanics and maintenance of one's firearm.

Proficiency is not solely about shooting; it is also about ensuring the tool being used is in optimal condition. This includes regular cleaning, proper lubrication, and a thorough understanding of how the firearm functions. Familiarity with common wear points and potential failure points allows a shooter to proactively address issues before they manifest as malfunctions during critical moments. Attending armorer's courses or seeking out detailed instructional materials on firearm maintenance can significantly enhance a shooter's confidence in their equipment and their ability to keep it running reliably. This knowledge base contributes to a holistic approach to firearm competency, where the shooter and their equipment are both in a state of readiness.

The integration of mental conditioning with physical practice is also paramount. Firearms competency is as much a mental game as it is a physical one. Developing resilience to stress, practicing controlled breathing techniques, and cultivating a mindset of proactive vigilance are all integral components of continuous training. This might involve visualization exercises, where shooters mentally rehearse scenarios and their responses, or it could involve participating in drills designed to simulate the psychological pressures of a defensive encounter.

The ability to remain calm, focused, and decisive when faced with a threat is a skill that can be developed and strengthened through dedicated mental training, complementing the physical drills performed on the range.

The journey of continuous training also involves a commitment to staying informed about evolving best practices and emerging threats. The world of personal defense and security is not static. New techniques, technologies, and legal considerations are constantly being introduced. Engaging with reputable instructors, reading relevant literature from credible sources, and participating in professional development opportunities ensures that a shooter's knowledge and skills remain current and relevant. This intellectual engagement with the subject matter fosters a deeper understanding and a more adaptable approach to firearm use.

Ultimately, the philosophy of continuous training is rooted in the understanding that responsible firearm ownership is a lifelong commitment. It is a commitment to oneself, to one's loved ones, and to the community to be as prepared and as competent as possible. It is a recognition that proficiency is not a one-time achievement, but a discipline that requires consistent dedication. By embracing regular practice, pursuing advanced education, engaging in dry-fire drills, understanding firearm mechanics, and cultivating mental resilience, firearm owners can ensure that their skills remain sharp, their confidence is well-founded, and they are truly prepared to meet the responsibilities that come with firearm ownership. This ongoing process is the true path to mastery and the hallmark of a truly competent and responsible individual.

Legal Preparedness Navigating the Law with Confidence

Legal preparedness is an indispensable facet of responsible firearm ownership, standing shoulder-to-shoulder with marksmanship and tactical proficiency. It is not an afterthought but a foundational element, ensuring that one's actions, even in the most dire circumstances, align with the law and ethical conduct. To carry a firearm for self-defense is to accept a profound responsibility, one that extends far beyond the ability to accurately engage a target. It encompasses a deep understanding of the legal landscape that governs the use of force, particularly deadly force. This knowledge is not merely academic; it is a vital shield that protects the responsible gun owner from potential legal repercussions, ensuring that a justifiable act of self-preservation does not inadvertently lead to criminal charges or civil liability.

At the heart of legal preparedness lies an intimate knowledge of your local jurisdiction's laws concerning the use of force.

These laws are not uniform across states or even municipalities, and what is permissible in one area may be illegal in another. The concept of "justifiable use of force" is paramount. In essence, it dictates that the use of force, and especially deadly force, must be necessary to prevent imminent death or great bodily harm to oneself or another innocent person. This necessity is the bedrock of any self-defense claim. It means that the threat must be immediate and severe. A perceived future threat, or a threat that can be reasonably avoided through other means, generally does not meet the legal threshold for the justifiable use of deadly force. Understanding the nuances of "imminence" and "great bodily harm" as defined by your local statutes is critical. This often involves extensive study of case law and statutory interpretation, as these terms can be subject to interpretation by legal professionals and juries.

One of the most significant legal principles to grasp is the "duty to retreat." In some jurisdictions, you may have a legal obligation to retreat if you can do so safely before resorting to deadly force. This duty typically applies when you are not in your own home. The concept of "Castle Doctrine" is a crucial counterpoint to the duty to retreat, particularly in states that have adopted it. The Castle Doctrine often presumes that you have no duty to retreat when you are in your own home, and in some states, this protection extends to your vehicle or even your workplace. However, the specifics of these doctrines vary widely. Some states may require you to have a reasonable belief that retreat would be dangerous before you can use force. Others may eliminate the duty to retreat entirely, allowing for the use of force if you are lawfully present and reasonably believe it is necessary. Ignorance of your state's specific stance on the duty to retreat and the Castle Doctrine can have dire consequences.

The legal ramifications of using a firearm in self-defense are extensive and can extend far beyond the immediate aftermath of an incident. Even if your actions are deemed legally justifiable, you will almost certainly face a thorough investigation by law enforcement. This investigation will scrutinize every aspect of the encounter, from the events leading up to it to the precise manner in which force was employed. Beyond the criminal investigation, there is the potential for civil lawsuits. An assailant, or their family, could sue for damages, even if you were acquitted of criminal charges. This is where the importance of having adequate liability insurance becomes evident. Such insurance can help cover the substantial costs associated with legal defense, both criminal and civil, which can quickly run into tens of thousands of dollars.

Beyond the statutes and case law, ethical considerations play a significant role in how the legal system views the use of force. The law, while defining the boundaries, often aligns with societal expectations of responsible behavior. This is where the concept of "proportionality" comes into play. The force used must be proportional to the threat faced. Using deadly force to stop a minor offense, such as petty theft where no physical harm is threatened, is unlikely to be deemed justifiable. The legal system, and the public perception it reflects, generally expects that deadly force will only be employed when facing a threat of death or grievous injury. This reinforces the importance of having a clear, rational assessment of the threat before resorting to lethal means.

De-escalation is not merely a tactical suggestion; it is a critical component of legal preparedness. Whenever possible, avoiding a confrontation is the safest and most legally sound course of action. This involves employing verbal de-escalation techniques, creating distance, and seeking opportunities to disengage from a potentially volatile situation. The law generally favors those who have made reasonable efforts to avoid violence. If a situation can be resolved through dialogue, or by simply leaving the area, your legal standing will be significantly stronger if you can demonstrate that you pursued these avenues before resorting to the use of force. It is also crucial to understand that your actions after an incident are just as important as your actions during it.

Following a self-defense incident, your immediate actions are crucial for both your safety and your legal protection. The first and most important step is to call emergency services. Clearly state that you have been the victim of an attack and that you have used force in self-defense. If possible and safe to do so, identify yourself to the responding officers. Avoid discussing the specifics of the incident in detail with anyone other than law enforcement and your legal counsel. Anything you say can and will be used against you, even if your intentions are to explain your actions. Do not offer unsolicited opinions, speculate about the assailant's intentions, or engage in arguments with witnesses. It is wise to remain silent on the details of the event until you have had the opportunity to consult with an attorney.

The role of an attorney in these situations cannot be overstated. If you carry a firearm for self-defense, it is highly advisable to consult with an attorney who specializes in self-defense law. This attorney can provide invaluable guidance on your local laws, explain the potential legal ramifications, and, most importantly, be a point of contact if you ever find yourself in a situation where you must use force.

Some legal defense funds and organizations offer affordable legal representation for their members, which can be a wise investment for any responsible gun owner. Knowing who to call and having that relationship established *before* an incident occurs can be a critical advantage.

Furthermore, understanding the nuances of "reasonable belief" is fundamental. The law often centers on whether your belief that you were in imminent danger of death or great bodily harm was *reasonable* under the circumstances. This involves considering what a reasonable person, in your situation, with your knowledge, and under the same circumstances, would have believed. This standard is subjective to a degree, but it is ultimately judged by an objective criterion. Factors such as the assailant's actions, words, demeanor, size, number, and whether they were armed all contribute to what constitutes a reasonable belief. This underscores the importance of being observant and aware of your surroundings at all times, not just for tactical reasons, but also to build a solid foundation for a potential self-defense claim.

The concept of "unlawful or excessive force" is also a critical legal boundary. While you are justified in using force to defend yourself, that force must not be excessive. For example, if an assailant is subdued and no longer a threat, continuing to use force against them would be unlawful and could result in criminal charges. This applies even in the heat of the moment; the force used must cease when the threat ceases. This principle reinforces the need for control and a clear understanding of when the threat has been neutralized.

Finally, responsible firearm ownership is a continuous learning process, and legal preparedness is no exception. Laws can change, and interpretations can evolve. Staying informed through reputable sources, attending legal seminars focused on self-defense, and regularly reviewing your understanding of your local statutes are all part of this ongoing commitment. It is not enough to know the law; one must also understand how it is applied and how it might be applied to their specific circumstances. This proactive approach ensures that your ability to defend yourself is not only physically and mentally sharp but also legally sound, providing true peace of mind in your commitment to self-protection.

Mental Readiness and Emotional Control

The adage that a firearm is only as effective as the mind behind it rings profoundly true, especially when we delve into the critical domain of mental readiness and emotional control. While the preceding discussions have focused on the tangible aspects of firearm competency – the legal frameworks, the ethical considerations, and the physical mechanics of safe and effective handling – this section shifts our gaze inward, to the psychological landscape that underpins every decision and action involving a defensive tool. To truly commit to lifelong firearm competency is to embark on a journey of cultivating a robust mental fortitude, a disciplined emotional compass, and an unwavering capacity for clear, decisive action, even when faced with the most extreme duress.

The reality of self-defense scenarios, particularly those that might necessitate the use of a firearm, is that they are intrinsically tied to heightened states of stress and emotional turmoil. The human body's primal response to perceived threat – the "fight or flight" mechanism – is a powerful physiological cascade designed for survival. While this system is remarkably effective at preserving life in immediate, instinctual situations, it can also lead to a host of detrimental effects on cognitive function and fine motor skills when not properly understood and managed. This is where the proactive cultivation of mental readiness becomes not just an advantage, but a necessity. It's about understanding your own psychological responses and developing strategies to mitigate their negative impacts, ensuring that your training and preparedness translate into effective action when it matters most.

Situational awareness, often referred to as "the first line of defense," is the bedrock of mental readiness. It is the continuous, conscious process of observing and processing your surroundings to identify potential threats and understand the dynamics of your environment. This isn't about paranoia; it's about prudent vigilance. It involves developing a keen eye for anomalies, for things that are out of place, for behaviors that deviate from the norm. This includes not only observing people and their actions but also understanding the geography of your surroundings – exits, cover, potential obstacles, and the general flow of activity. Cultivating situational awareness is an active, ongoing practice. It requires deliberate effort to shift from a passive, absorbing state to an alert, analytical one. This means consciously scanning your environment in public places, noting who is around you, what they are doing, and how they are behaving. It involves identifying potential escape routes, understanding the layout of buildings, and being aware of the general mood or tension in a particular area. Developing this habit can significantly reduce the likelihood of being caught off guard, providing precious moments to assess, evade, or prepare.

Beyond simply observing, true situational awareness involves a process of evaluation. What are you seeing? What does it mean? What are the potential implications?

This is where the mind begins to act as a sophisticated threat-detection system. It involves recognizing patterns of behavior that might indicate ill intent, such as individuals loitering suspiciously, exhibiting excessive nervousness, or engaging in actions that seem out of context. It also involves understanding the "normal" baseline of a situation and then identifying deviations from that baseline. For example, in a quiet park, a sudden surge of loud, aggressive behavior might be a red flag. In a crowded marketplace, however, a certain level of ambient noise and movement is expected. The ability to quickly differentiate between the mundane and the potentially threatening is a skill that can be honed through conscious practice and reflection.

The mental preparation for potential threats extends to building a mental model of what a self-defense encounter might entail. This isn't about fantasizing about violent confrontations, but rather about realistically visualizing scenarios and considering your potential responses. This can involve mental rehearsals of actions such as drawing your firearm, aiming, and engaging a target, all within the context of a stressful situation. This type of mental rehearsal, often employed by athletes and military personnel, can help to reduce the cognitive load during an actual event.

By mentally practicing the sequence of actions, you are essentially pre-programming your brain and body, making the physical execution more fluid and less prone to error when under pressure. This also includes anticipating the likely actions of an aggressor and planning your own countermeasures.

A critical component of mental readiness is the development of what is often termed a "decisive mindset." In a high-stress situation, hesitation can be as dangerous as an incorrect action. A decisive mindset involves the ability to process information rapidly, make a judgment, and act upon that judgment with conviction. This is not about rashness, but about confident decision-making based on the best available information under adverse conditions. This confidence is built through rigorous training, consistent practice, and a deep understanding of your capabilities and limitations. When you have trained extensively and know your firearm, your tactics, and your legal responsibilities intimately, you are far more likely to make sound decisions under duress. The uncertainty that can plague an untrained individual is replaced by a calculated confidence born from preparation.

The emotional impact of using a firearm in self-defense is profound and cannot be overstated. Even when the use of force is legally justifiable and morally sound, the act of taking a life, or even the intent to do so, carries a significant psychological weight. Responsible firearm owners must acknowledge and prepare for these emotional consequences. This involves understanding that post-incident emotional distress, such as shock, fear, guilt, or even a sense of detachment, is a normal human response. These feelings can manifest in various ways, from nightmares and anxiety to difficulty concentrating and social withdrawal.

Preparing for this emotional fallout is as important as preparing for the physical encounter. This might involve discussing these potential impacts with trusted friends, family, or mental health professionals *before* any incident occurs. Knowing that these emotions are a common and expected reaction can help to normalize the experience and make it easier to cope with. Seeking support is not a sign of weakness; it is a testament to one's commitment to comprehensive well-being and responsible conduct. It ensures that the act of self-preservation does not lead to long-term psychological harm.

Managing stress and its physiological manifestations is a core element of emotional control. The elevated heart rate, rapid breathing, tunnel vision, and auditory exclusion that often accompany high-stress events can severely impair performance.

Training methodologies that simulate these stress responses, such as force-on-force training or shooting under timed, challenging conditions, can help individuals learn to perform effectively *despite* these physiological changes. This is often referred to as "stress inoculation." By repeatedly exposing yourself to controlled stressors, your body and mind adapt, becoming more resilient and less susceptible to incapacitation. The goal is not to eliminate the stress response entirely – that's impossible – but to learn to channel it, to maintain enough cognitive function to execute necessary actions.

This might involve practicing specific breathing techniques to regulate heart rate and calm the nervous system. Simple exercises like controlled, deep breaths can have a significant impact on stress levels. Furthermore, developing mental anchors or mantras can help to refocus the mind when it begins to stray into unproductive emotional territory. These can be simple phrases that remind you of your training, your purpose, or your commitment to controlled action. For example, a phrase like "control the breath, control the shot" can serve as a powerful reminder to maintain composure under fire.

The concept of "responsible decision-making under duress" is the intersection of mental readiness, emotional control, and legal preparedness.

It is the ability to quickly assess a threat, weigh the legal and ethical implications of your actions, and make a choice that is both effective for your self-preservation and legally defensible. This requires a deep internalisation of legal statutes, particularly those concerning the use of force. When faced with a threat, the untrained mind might react purely on instinct. The trained mind, however, has integrated the legal framework into its decision-making process. It understands the concept of "imminent threat," the "duty to retreat" (if applicable), and the principle of "proportionality."

This integration doesn't happen instantaneously in the heat of the moment. It requires consistent, conscious effort during training. Scenarios should be designed not just to test marksmanship but also to force the student to make critical decisions that have legal and ethical ramifications. For example, a scenario might present a seemingly threatening individual who ultimately backs down. The student must then make the decision to cease their defensive posture, to de-escalate, and to avoid unnecessary escalation, even if they were initially justified in perceiving a threat. This reinforces the understanding that the right to self-defense is not a license to initiate or prolong conflict.

The development of mental fortitude is a lifelong commitment. It's not a destination, but an ongoing process of self-improvement and refinement. This involves a willingness to confront uncomfortable truths about oneself and one's reactions to stress. It requires humility to acknowledge areas of weakness and a dedication to continuous learning and practice. This might include seeking out advanced training, participating in realistic scenario-based exercises, and engaging in regular mental self-assessment. Reflecting on training sessions, analyzing what went well and what could be improved, is a crucial part of this process.

Furthermore, maintaining physical health plays a significant role in mental and emotional resilience. Adequate sleep, proper nutrition, and regular physical exercise contribute to a body that is better equipped to handle stress. The physical symptoms of stress can be exacerbated by poor physical condition. A body that is well-nourished and conditioned will be more resilient to the physiological demands of a high-stress event. This interconnectedness underscores the holistic nature of firearm competency. It is not just about the gun; it is about the entire person.

In essence, the mental and emotional dimensions of firearm competency are about building a reservoir of control and clarity that can withstand the storm of a violent encounter. It's about cultivating the discipline to maintain situational awareness even when distracted, the emotional resilience to manage fear and anxiety, and the cognitive clarity to make sound, ethical, and legal decisions under extreme pressure. This is the ultimate expression of responsible firearm ownership – not just the ability to deploy a tool effectively, but the wisdom and self-mastery to do so only when absolutely necessary, and to do so with precision, restraint, and a clear understanding of the profound gravity of the action. This mental and emotional preparedness is the invisible, yet indispensable, component that elevates a mere gun owner to a truly competent and responsible protector.

Selecting a Qualified Instructor Investing in Your Skill

The journey toward lifelong firearm competency is a multi-faceted endeavor, extending far beyond the mere acquisition of a firearm and a basic understanding of its operation. While legal knowledge and the cultivation of mental and emotional resilience, as discussed previously, form crucial pillars of responsible ownership, the practical application and refinement of skills are paramount. This development is not an insular pursuit; it thrives on expert guidance.

Selecting a qualified instructor is not just a recommendation; it is an investment in your safety, your proficiency, and your ultimate confidence in handling a defensive tool. The caliber of your instruction will directly influence the speed and effectiveness of your skill acquisition, shaping your habits and potentially your life-saving capabilities in a critical moment. Therefore, the process of choosing an instructor warrants careful consideration, akin to selecting a mentor for any other high-stakes profession.

The landscape of firearm instruction is varied, populated by individuals with differing backgrounds, methodologies, and levels of expertise. To navigate this terrain effectively, it is essential to establish a set of criteria by which to evaluate potential instructors. Foremost among these is the instructor's credentials and certifications. Reputable organizations dedicated to firearm safety and training often offer certification programs that attest to an instructor's knowledge base and their ability to impart that knowledge safely and effectively. Look for instructors certified by well-established and respected entities within the firearm training community. These certifications often require rigorous testing, adherence to a specific code of conduct, and ongoing professional development, ensuring that the instructor remains current with best practices and evolving safety standards. While a certification is a strong indicator, it is not the sole determinant of quality. Many highly skilled and experienced instructors may have developed their expertise through extensive practical application and mentorship rather than formal certification. However, for the beginner, a recognized certification provides a valuable baseline assurance of foundational competence.

Beyond formal certifications, the instructor's experience is a critical factor. How long have they been teaching? What types of students do they typically train? An instructor who has worked with a diverse range of individuals, from complete novices to seasoned professionals, will possess a broader understanding of learning challenges and a more adaptable teaching style. Consider their background: are they former law enforcement, military personnel, or competitive shooters? Each of these backgrounds can bring a unique perspective and skill set to the training. However, it is crucial to distinguish between experience in using firearms and experience in *teaching* others to use them. A decorated marksman may be an exceptional shooter, but that does not automatically translate into an ability to break down complex concepts into digestible lessons for a beginner. The best instructors are not only skilled practitioners but also effective communicators and educators.

Safety is the absolute bedrock of firearm instruction. A qualified instructor will place an unwavering emphasis on safety protocols, demonstrating a deep respect for firearms and a commitment to fostering safe habits in their students. During initial interactions or introductory sessions, observe their attitude towards safety. Do they consistently enforce muzzle discipline, proper handling techniques, and a thorough understanding of the four universal firearm safety rules? Their range commands should be clear, concise, and consistently applied. A reputable instructor will not only demonstrate safe practices but will actively correct unsafe behavior immediately and constructively. Moreover, their own safety record is a testament to their competence. Inquire about their training facility's safety record and be wary of any instructor who seems cavalier about safety procedures or dismisses concerns. A pristine safety record, both personally and within their training operations, is a non-negotiable requirement.

An instructor's teaching philosophy and methodology are also vital considerations. Different instructors will approach the learning process in distinct ways. Some may favor a highly structured, step-by-step approach, breaking down each skill into minute components. Others might adopt a more intuitive or "holistic" method, emphasizing the overall feel and flow of the action. The ideal approach for you will depend on your individual learning style, your prior experience, and your personal goals. Do you learn best through repetition and detailed instruction, or do you thrive in a more dynamic, scenario-based environment? A good instructor will be able to articulate their teaching philosophy clearly and will be willing to adapt their methods to suit your needs. Don't hesitate to ask about their curriculum, their approach to common challenges, and how they measure student progress. A transparent and student-centered philosophy is a strong indicator of a dedicated educator.

The ability to communicate effectively is arguably the most crucial attribute of a qualified instructor. Firearm instruction involves the transfer of complex physical and cognitive skills, often under circumstances that can induce stress and anxiety. An instructor must be able to explain concepts clearly, patiently, and in a manner that resonates with the student. This includes being able to break down intricate techniques into simple, understandable steps. They should be adept at providing constructive feedback, identifying areas for improvement without discouraging the student, and offering solutions to overcome obstacles.

A truly effective instructor will possess empathy, understanding that many students may be experiencing fear, apprehension, or a lack of confidence. They should create a supportive learning environment where questions are encouraged, and mistakes are viewed as learning opportunities. If you find yourself struggling to understand an instructor's explanations or feeling intimidated by their demeanor, it is a sign that their communication style may not be the right fit for you.

When evaluating potential instructors, consider their specialization. While some instructors may offer a broad range of training, others may focus on specific areas such as concealed carry, competitive shooting, tactical applications, or basic handgun proficiency. If you have a particular goal in mind, such as obtaining a concealed carry permit or preparing for a specific type of shooting sport, seeking an instructor with expertise in that niche can be highly beneficial. They will be better equipped to tailor the training to your specific needs and provide insights relevant to your chosen path. However, for foundational competency, a generalist instructor with a strong emphasis on safety and fundamental skills is an excellent starting point.

The learning environment itself is another important aspect to assess. Is the training conducted in a safe, well-maintained facility? Whether it's a live-fire range or a classroom setting, the environment should be conducive to learning and free from distractions. A professional instructor will ensure that the equipment they use is in good condition, that the range is properly managed, and that all safety protocols are rigorously followed. For live-fire training, the availability of appropriate firearms for students to use, if needed, can be a significant advantage, especially for beginners who may not yet own their own firearm. The instructor's ability to provide or recommend appropriate training aids, such as dry-fire training tools, simulation software, or realistic target systems, can also enhance the learning experience.

It is also wise to seek testimonials or references from previous students. While not always readily available, a reputable instructor will likely have a positive reputation within the local firearm community. Online reviews, recommendations from trusted friends or family members, or even inquiries at local gun shops or ranges can provide valuable insights into an instructor's effectiveness and teaching style. Hearing about the experiences of others can help you gauge whether an instructor's approach aligns with your expectations and learning preferences.

Furthermore, consider the instructor's commitment to ongoing education and their professional development.

The field of firearm instruction, like many others, is constantly evolving with new research, technologies, and training methodologies emerging. An instructor who actively participates in advanced training, attends industry conferences, and stays current with best practices demonstrates a dedication to their craft and a commitment to providing the highest quality instruction. This continuous learning translates into more effective and up-to-date training for their students.

Ultimately, selecting a qualified instructor is about finding a partner in your pursuit of firearm competency. It's about finding someone who not only possesses the knowledge and skills to teach you effectively but also inspires confidence, fosters a safe learning environment, and adapts to your individual needs. It requires a proactive approach on your part to research, ask questions, and assess your options. Do not settle for the first instructor you encounter. Invest the time and effort to find someone who will provide you with a solid foundation, nurture your skills, and empower you to become a safe, confident, and responsible firearm owner. This commitment to finding the right guidance is an integral part of the lifelong journey of firearm competency, ensuring that your skills are honed under expert tutelage, preparing you for any eventuality with competence and assurance.

The Responsible Firearm Owners Pledge

The journey toward becoming a truly competent and responsible firearm owner is not a destination, but a continuous path of learning, practice, and unwavering commitment. We have explored the fundamental principles of safety, the importance of legal knowledge, the critical role of mental and emotional resilience, and the indispensable value of expert instruction. Now, as we reach the culmination of this chapter, it is essential to translate these concepts into a tangible, personal declaration – a pledge that embodies the enduring responsibilities that come with firearm ownership. This is not merely a symbolic gesture, but a deeply ingrained mindset that will guide your actions and ensure you uphold the highest standards of safety, proficiency, and ethical conduct throughout your life.

This pledge is a personal covenant with yourself, with your community, and with the principles of responsible gun ownership. It is a commitment that begins the moment you decide to own a firearm and continues for as long as you possess one. It is built upon the foundational pillars we have already discussed, interwoven with a proactive approach to maintaining and enhancing your capabilities. By internalizing and living by this pledge, you solidify your role not just as a firearm owner, but as a guardian of safety and a responsible member of society. It is a declaration that transcends casual possession and elevates ownership to a state of dedicated stewardship.

The first and most critical element of this pledge is an unyielding commitment to absolute safety. This means embracing the Four Universal Firearm Safety Rules not as suggestions, but as inviolable commandments: Treat every firearm as if it were loaded. Never point the muzzle at anything you are not willing to destroy. Keep your finger off the trigger until your sights are on the target and you have decided to fire. Be sure of your target and what is beyond it. This commitment extends beyond these rules to encompass a constant vigilance in handling, storage, and maintenance. It means ensuring your firearms are always secured when not under your direct supervision, preventing unauthorized access by children or individuals who are not trained or authorized to use them. It involves diligent inspection of your firearms before and after each use, verifying their condition and functionality, and meticulously cleaning and lubricating them according to manufacturer guidelines. Safety is not a passive state; it is an active, daily practice. It is the ingrained habit of checking your action before holstering, the mindful placement of your firearm during a range break, and the conscious awareness of your surroundings at all times when handling a firearm. This pledge means that safety is never an afterthought; it is the primary consideration in every interaction you have with a firearm.

Secondly, your pledge must include a dedication to continuous learning and skill refinement. The world of firearms and self-defense is dynamic, with evolving technologies, training methodologies, and legal landscapes. Your commitment to competency must be lifelong. This means actively seeking out advanced training opportunities beyond the initial introduction. It involves regularly attending workshops, taking specialized courses, and engaging with qualified instructors who can challenge your existing skills and introduce new techniques. It also means dedicating time to consistent practice, not just on the range, but also through dry-fire exercises at home. Proficiency is not maintained by chance; it is cultivated through deliberate and consistent effort. This extends to staying informed about the latest developments in firearm technology, defensive tactics, and, critically, the laws governing firearm ownership and use in your jurisdiction. Your pledge is to remain a student of the craft, always seeking to improve your knowledge and abilities. It means actively engaging with resources that promote skill development, whether through reputable books, online courses, or professional training organizations.

Thirdly, a cornerstone of this pledge is an unwavering commitment to legal adherence and ethical conduct. The right to bear arms comes with profound responsibilities. Your pledge must explicitly state your commitment to understanding and obeying all federal, state, and local laws pertaining to firearm ownership, possession, transfer, and use. This includes, but is not limited to, laws regarding concealed carry permits, background checks, prohibited persons, and the legal justification for the use of deadly force. Ignorance of the law is not a defense, and your pledge acknowledges this reality. Beyond legal compliance, your commitment must encompass an ethical framework. This means using a firearm only as a last resort, when all other reasonable options for de-escalation or escape have been exhausted, and only when there is a clear and present danger of death or serious bodily harm to yourself or others. It means understanding the gravity of taking a human life and being prepared for the legal, psychological, and emotional ramifications of such an act. Your pledge is to be a responsible citizen who respects the law and wields this potent tool with wisdom and restraint. This includes understanding the nuances of justified force and the severe consequences of its misuse.

Furthermore, your pledge should encompass a commitment to responsible storage and access prevention. This is a critical component of safety and community well-being. It means ensuring that your firearms are stored in a manner that prevents unauthorized access, particularly by children, individuals who are legally prohibited from owning firearms, or those who may be experiencing a mental health crisis. This often involves the use of gun safes, locking devices, and the separation of ammunition from the firearm. Your pledge is to make responsible storage a non-negotiable aspect of your firearm ownership, recognizing the immense responsibility you have to prevent accidents and misuse. This commitment extends to understanding the varying needs of safe storage based on your living situation and family composition and actively implementing the most effective solutions.

Your pledge also implies a commitment to advocacy for responsible gun ownership. As a responsible owner, you are an ambassador for the shooting community. Your actions, your knowledge, and your dedication to safety speak volumes. Your pledge is to represent responsible gun ownership positively through your conduct and to educate others about the importance of safety, training, and legal compliance.

This may involve engaging in constructive conversations, sharing accurate information, and supporting organizations that promote gun safety and responsible firearm practices. It is about being a force for good within the broader discourse surrounding firearms.

Finally, this pledge is a commitment to self-awareness and emotional preparedness. Owning a firearm, especially for self-defense, carries a significant psychological burden. Your pledge is to be aware of your own emotional state, to understand your triggers, and to seek help if you are struggling with stress, anger, or any other condition that could impair your judgment or your ability to handle a firearm safely and responsibly. It involves acknowledging the immense mental fortitude required in a high-stress situation and proactively working to maintain your emotional equilibrium. This may involve seeking professional counseling or engaging in mindfulness practices. Your pledge is to ensure that you are not only technically proficient but also mentally and emotionally ready for the immense responsibility that firearm ownership entails. It is a holistic approach to preparedness, recognizing that the mind is as crucial a tool as the firearm itself.

To fully embody this pledge, consider writing it down, perhaps even signing and dating it.

Keep it in a place where you will see it regularly, perhaps near where you store your firearms, as a constant reminder of your dedication. This personal declaration is more than just words; it is a solemn vow to uphold the principles that define a responsible firearm owner. It is the final, yet ongoing, step in your lifelong commitment to firearm competency and stewardship. By embracing this pledge, you ensure that your ownership of a firearm is not just a right exercised, but a profound responsibility honored, contributing to a safer self and a safer community. This is the enduring legacy of a truly responsible gun owner.

Appendix

This appendix provides supplementary materials and resources to enhance your understanding and practice of responsible firearm ownership. It includes a comprehensive checklist for firearm safety, a guide to understanding basic firearm maintenance. Additionally, you will find a template for a personal firearm safety pledge, which you are encouraged to adapt and personalize. It is important to consult these resources regularly as you continue your journey in firearm competency.

Comprehensive Firearm Safety Checklist
I. Core Firearm Safety Rules (Non-Negotiable)

☐ Treat every firearm as loaded at all times
☐ Never point a firearm at anything you are not willing to destroy
☐ Keep your finger off the trigger until sights are on target and you have decided to fire
☐ Be sure of your target, what is around it, and what is beyond it

Failure to follow any one of these rules can result in serious injury or death.

II. Personal Responsibility & Readiness

☐ You are legally authorized to possess and carry the firearm
☐ You are properly trained and qualified for this firearm
☐ You are physically and mentally fit to carry and use a firearm
☐ You are not under the influence of alcohol, drugs, or impairing medication

- ☐ You understand your legal authority and use-of-force limitations
- ☐ You know when not to use a firearm

III. Firearm Condition Check (Before Handling)

- ☐ Point firearm in a safe direction
- ☐ Remove magazine (if applicable)
- ☐ Lock action open
- ☐ Visually inspect chamber
- ☐ Physically inspect chamber
- ☐ Verify firearm is unloaded
- ☐ Confirm correct caliber ammunition for the firearm
- ☐ Check safety mechanisms (if applicable)

Never rely solely on a safety lever or mechanical device.

IV. Ammunition Safety

- ☐ Use only manufacturer-approved ammunition
- ☐ Verify correct caliber and cartridge type
- ☐ Inspect ammunition for defects (cracks, corrosion, dents)
- ☐ Do not mix ammunition types
- ☐ Store ammunition separately when appropriate
- ☐ Never chamber damaged or questionable ammunition

V. Safe Loading Procedures

- ☐ Firearm pointed in a safe direction
- ☐ Finger off trigger
- ☐ Insert magazine or load cylinder properly
- ☐ Chamber round only when authorized and necessary
- ☐ Engage safety or decock if applicable
- ☐ Confirm firearm status after loading

VI. Safe Carry Practices

☐ Use an approved holster that covers the trigger guard
☐ Holster allows secure retention
☐ Holster is appropriate for firearm type
☐ Firearm secured against unauthorized access
☐ No manual manipulation of trigger while holstering
☐ Avoid unnecessary handling or "adjusting" the firearm

VII. Drawing and Re-Holstering Safety

☐ Finger indexed along frame during draw
☐ Muzzle discipline maintained at all times
☐ Draw only when legally and tactically justified
☐ Re-holster slowly and deliberately
☐ Visually confirm holster is clear
☐ Never force firearm into holster

VIII. Use-of-Force Decision Safety

☐ Deadly force is legally justified
☐ Threat is imminent and unavoidable
☐ No reasonable lesser alternative exists
☐ You understand you are responsible for every round fired
☐ You are aware of bystanders and backdrop
☐ You can articulate your decision

If you cannot justify firing, do not fire.

IX. Malfunctions & Stoppages

☐ Maintain muzzle discipline
☐ Finger off trigger
☐ Identify malfunction safely
☐ Follow trained clearance procedures
☐ If unsure, unload and secure firearm
☐ Seek qualified assistance if needed

X. Post-Incident Safety Procedures

☐ Scan for additional threats
☐ Finger off trigger
☐ Maintain muzzle discipline
☐ Secure firearm as trained
☐ Do not tamper with evidence
☐ Comply with lawful commands
☐ Render aid if safe and trained to do so
☐ Document incident accurately

XI. Storage & Transport Safety

☐ Firearm unloaded when required
☐ Use approved locking device or safe
☐ Store firearms inaccessible to unauthorized persons
☐ Transport firearms according to law and policy
☐ Separate ammunition when appropriate
☐ Secure firearms in vehicles properly

XII. Cleaning & Maintenance Safety

☐ Firearm unloaded before cleaning
☐ Chamber verified visually and physically
☐ Ammunition removed from cleaning area
☐ Follow manufacturer cleaning procedures
☐ Inspect firearm after reassembly
☐ Function check completed safely

XIII. Range Safety Checklist

☐ Follow all range rules and commands
☐ Wear eye and ear protection
☐ Fire only on command
☐ Cease fire immediately when directed
☐ Keep firearm unloaded during cease fire
☐ Never cross firing line without permission
☐ Handle malfunctions safely

XIV. Prohibited Actions (Always Unsafe)

☒ Horseplay or joking with firearms
☒ Pointing firearms at people as a "joke"
☒ Trigger finger while moving or searching
☒ Unauthorized modifications
☒ Alcohol or drugs with firearms
☒ Ignoring safety violations by others

XV. Ongoing Safety Responsibilities

☐ Maintain regular training and qualification
☐ Review use-of-force laws periodically
☐ Practice safe handling consistently

- ☐ Correct unsafe behavior immediately
- ☐ Report safety concerns or equipment issues
- ☐ Lead by example

Final Safety Principle

Firearm safety is not a checklist you complete once — it is a discipline you practice every time you touch a firearm.

A Guide to Understanding Basic Firearm Maintenance

Firearm maintenance is essential for **safe operation, reliability, and service life**. A poorly maintained firearm is more likely to malfunction, misfire, or fail at a critical moment. Basic maintenance ensures your firearm functions as designed and remain safe to handle.

1. Why Firearm Maintenance Matters

Proper maintenance helps to:

- Preventing malfunctions and stoppages
- Reduce wear and corrosion
- Maintain accuracy and reliability
- Detect mechanical issues early
- Ensure safe operation during carry and use

Maintenance is a safety responsibility, not just a mechanical task.

2. Firearm Safety Before Maintenance (Always First)

Before any maintenance begins:

☐ Point the firearm in a safe direction
☐ Remove the magazine (if applicable)
☐ Open and lock the action
☐ Visually inspect the chamber
☐ Physically inspect the chamber

- ☐ Verify the firearm is unloaded
- ☐ Remove all ammunition from the work area

Never rely on a safety lever alone.

3. Basic Components You Should Understand

While designs vary, most firearms include:

- **Barrel** – directs the projectile
- **Action** – loads, fires, extracts, and ejects ammunition
- **Trigger group** – initiates firing
- **Slide / Bolt / Cylinder** – varies by firearm type
- **Recoil system** – manages cycling and energy
- **Frame or Receiver** – main structural component

Understanding these parts helps you clean and inspect correctly.

4. Field Stripping (Basic Disassembly)

Field stripping is **limited disassembly** for routine cleaning and inspection. It does **not** involve detailed internal disassembly.

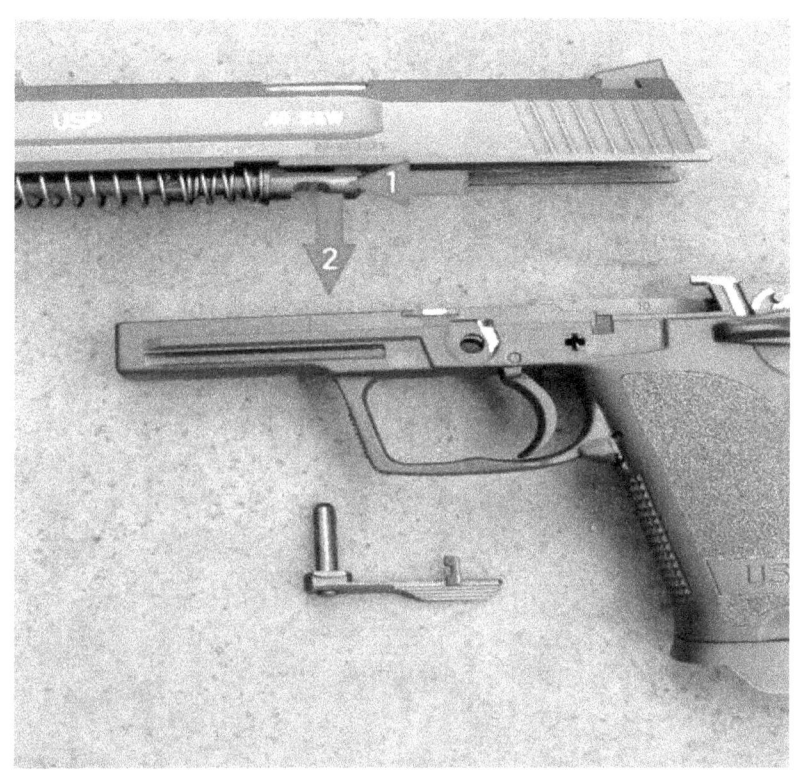

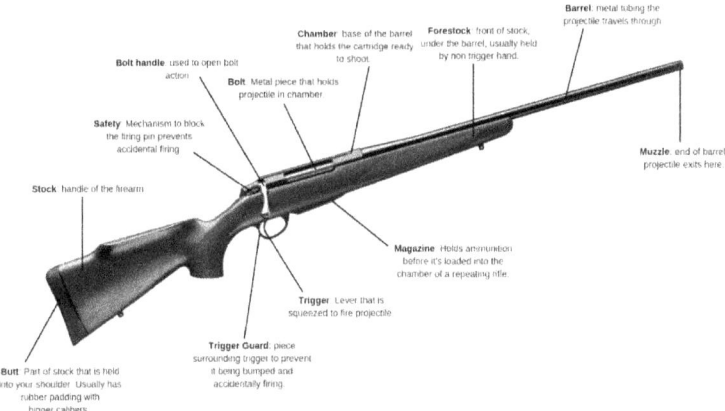

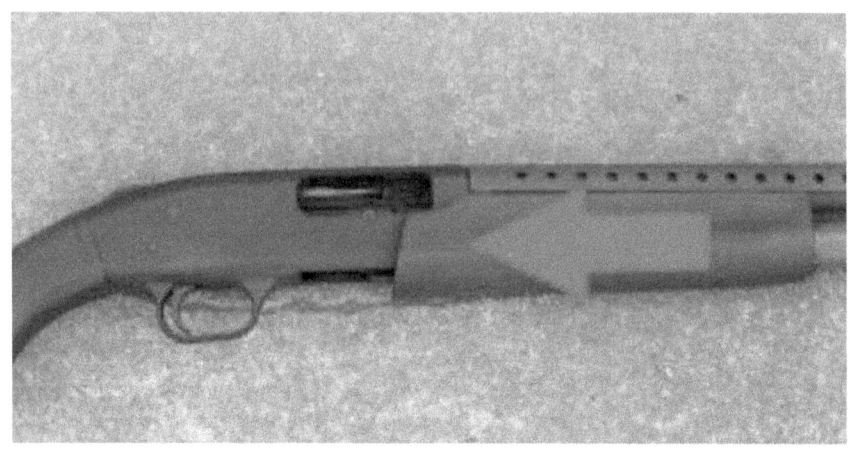

Key Rules for Field Stripping

- Follow the manufacturer's instructions
- Disassemble only to the level you were trained
- Stop if resistance or confusion occurs
- Never force components

If unsure, seek qualified assistance.

5. Cleaning the Firearm

A. Barrel Cleaning

- Use the correct caliber cleaning rod or bore snake
- Run solvent-soaked patches through the barrel
- Brush lightly if needed
- Follow with dry patches
- Lightly oil after cleaning

Always clean **from chamber to muzzle** when possible.

B. Action & Moving Parts

- Remove carbon, dirt, and debris
- Use nylon or brass brushes (not steel)
- Wipe parts clean with lint-free cloths
- Avoid excessive solvent soaking

C. Frame / Receiver

- Wipe down rails and contact points
- Remove visible debris
- Inspect for cracks or abnormal wear

6. Lubrication (Less Is More)

Proper lubrication reduces friction and wear.

Lubrication Guidelines

- Apply a small amount of oil
- Lubricate moving contact points only
- Avoid over-lubrication
- Wipe away excess oil

Too much oil attracts dirt and can cause malfunctions.

7. Inspection During Maintenance

Cleaning time is inspection time.

Check for:

- Cracks or fractures
- Excessive wear
- Loose screws or pins
- Deformed springs
- Rust or corrosion
- Damaged magazines

If defects are found, do not carry or fire the firearm until corrected.

8. Reassembly and Function Check

After cleaning:

☐ Reassemble according to manufacturer instructions
☐ Ensure all parts are seated correctly
☐ Perform a **function check** (without ammunition)
☐ Verify safeties and controls operate properly

Never skip the function check.

9. Cleaning Frequency Guidelines

General recommendations:

- After each range session
- After exposure to rain, sweat, or dirt

- Before long-term storage
- Periodically during regular carry

Duty or carry firearms require more frequent inspection.

10. Safe Storage After Maintenance

- Store unloaded unless policy requires otherwise
- Use a secure locking device or safe
- Store ammunition properly
- Protect against moisture and humidity

Proper storage prevents corrosion and unauthorized access.

11. What Basic Maintenance Does NOT Include

Basic firearm maintenance does **not** include:

- Modifying internal parts
- Altering trigger pull
- Filing or grinding components
- Replacing springs without training
- Gunsmith-level repairs

These tasks require a qualified armorer or gunsmith.

12. Common Maintenance Mistakes to Avoid

☒ Failing to verify unloaded status
☒ Over-lubricating
☒ Using incorrect tools
☒ Mixing firearm parts
☒ Ignoring wear or damage
☒ Cleaning in areas with live ammunition

Final Principle

A clean firearm is a safer, more reliable firearm—but only when cleaned correctly.

Basic maintenance is about:

- Safety
- Awareness
- Consistency
- Responsibility

Personal Firearm Safety Pledge

I, _____,
(Print Full Name)

recognize that firearm ownership and possession carry serious responsibilities. I commit to the highest standards of safety, judgment, and lawful conduct whenever I handle, carry, store, or transport a firearm.

By signing this pledge, I affirm the following:

Safety Commitment

☐ I will treat every firearm as if it is loaded at all times.
☐ I will never point a firearm at anything I do not intend to shoot.
☐ I will keep my finger off the trigger until my sights are on target and I have made the conscious decision to fire.
☐ I will always be aware of my target, surroundings, and what is beyond the target.

Responsibility & Judgment

☐ I will handle firearms only when physically and mentally fit to do so.
☐ I will never mix firearms with alcohol, drugs, or impairing substances.
☐ I will operate firearms only within the limits of my training, authority, and the law.
☐ I will seek additional training whenever my skills or knowledge need improvement.

Storage & Access

☐ I will store firearms securely to prevent unauthorized access.
☐ I will store firearms responsibly around children, guests, and vulnerable individuals.
☐ I will use approved locking devices, safes, or other security measures as appropriate.

Maintenance & Condition

☐ I will maintain my firearms in safe working condition.
☐ I will inspect firearms regularly for wear, damage, or malfunction.
☐ I will unload and verify firearms are safe before cleaning or maintenance.

Carry & Use

☐ I will carry firearms only when legally authorized to do so.
☐ I will use approved holsters and safe carry methods.
☐ I understand I am personally responsible for every round fired.
☐ I will use a firearm only as a last resort, when legally justified.

Accountability

☐ I will correct unsafe behavior immediately—my own or others'.
☐ I will report lost, stolen, or unsafe firearms as required.
☐ I understand that firearm safety is a continuous obligation, not a one-time agreement.

Affirmation

I understand that failure to follow firearm safety principles can result in serious injury, loss of life, criminal liability, civil consequences, and permanent harm. I accept full responsibility for my actions and commit to handling firearms with respect, care, and discipline at all times.

Signature: _____

Date: _____

Witness / Instructor (if applicable): _____

Acknowledgements

I would like to express my sincere gratitude to my family for their unwavering support and understanding throughout the creation of this work. Their patience and encouragement were invaluable. I also extend my thanks to the numerous students and colleagues who have contributed to my understanding of security principles and firearm education over the years. Their insights and experiences have shaped my perspective and enriched my knowledge base. Lastly, I am grateful to the publishers for providing a platform to share this important information with a wider audience.

Glossary

Action: The mechanical assembly of a firearm that loads, fires, and ejects a cartridge.

Ammunition: A complete projectile, including the projectile itself, propellant, and primer, used in a firearm.

Chamber: The part of a firearm's barrel that holds the cartridge.

Concealed Carry Permit: A license that allows an individual to carry a concealed firearm.

De-escalation: The process of attempting to prevent a dangerous situation from becoming more violent.

Dry-fire: The practice of cycling the action of a firearm without live ammunition, used for trigger control and mechanics practice.

Muzzle: The front end of the barrel of a firearm, from which the projectile exits.

Projectile: The bullet or shot fired from a firearm.

Propellant: The explosive substance (e.g., gunpowder) that propels a projectile from a firearm.

Range Break: A designated period during live-fire training when all firearms are made safe and the firing line is cleared.

Trigger: The mechanism of a firearm that, when pulled, initiates the firing sequence.

Universal Firearm Safety Rules: A set of fundamental safety guidelines for handling firearms.

References

- National Shooting Sports Foundation (NSSF)
- Gun Owners of America (GOA)
- Brady United Against Gun Violence
- Everytown for Gun Safety
- Bureau of Alcohol, Tobacco, Firearms and Explosives (ATF)
- State-specific firearm laws and statutes (as applicable to the reader's jurisdiction)
- Reputable firearm training manuals and publications

Author Biography

Dr. Nicholas Cooley, PhD, is a distinguished leader in security education, firearms training, and professional consulting, widely recognized for his depth of experience, academic rigor, and practical instructional approach. With decades of immersive, real-world experience across the security and protective services spectrum, Dr. Cooley has established himself as a respected authority in private security, investigative practices, and responsible firearm ownership.

Dr. Cooley is the Founder and Senior Instructor of North Florida Security Academy, as well as the Owner of Bulldog Training Academy & Consultants. Through these organizations, he has trained thousands of individuals nationwide in concealed carry, defensive handgun skills, and advanced firearms techniques, while also providing comprehensive education in private security operations and private investigation fundamentals.

A nationally certified instructor, Dr. Cooley holds credentials as a Nationally Certified Law Enforcement Instructor, in addition to multiple professional instructor certifications across firearms, security, and tactical disciplines. His instructional experience spans emergency medical services, private investigation, security management, and tactical training, allowing him to deliver instruction that is both legally grounded and operationally sound.

Dr. Cooley's academic background further distinguishes his expertise. He holds advanced degrees in Security Management, Corporate Training and Instructional Design, Business Administration, and Human Body Behavior and Counseling. This rare combination enables him to seamlessly integrate behavioral science, decision-making psychology, and human performance principles into security and firearms training, enhancing both skill development and judgment under stress.

In addition to his work with adult professionals, Dr. Cooley is a published children's firearm-safety author and the creator of a nationally unique educational program, *The Safety Choices Series*, a one-of-a-kind children's book series designed for ages 3 through 16. This series reflects his commitment to early, age-appropriate safety education, emphasizing responsibility, awareness, and informed decision-making around firearms.

Dr. Cooley's teaching philosophy emphasizes not only technical proficiency, but also ethics, mindset, accountability, and legal awareness. His approach equips students with the practical skills required for real-world application while reinforcing the professional judgment essential to effective security operations and responsible firearm ownership.

Contact the Author

Dr. Cooley may be contacted via email at bulldogtrainingacademy@gmail.com, or through his website at www.bulldogtrainingacademy.net.

www.ingramcontent.com/pod-product-compliance
Lightning Source LLC
Chambersburg PA
CBHW070634160426
43194CB00009B/1454